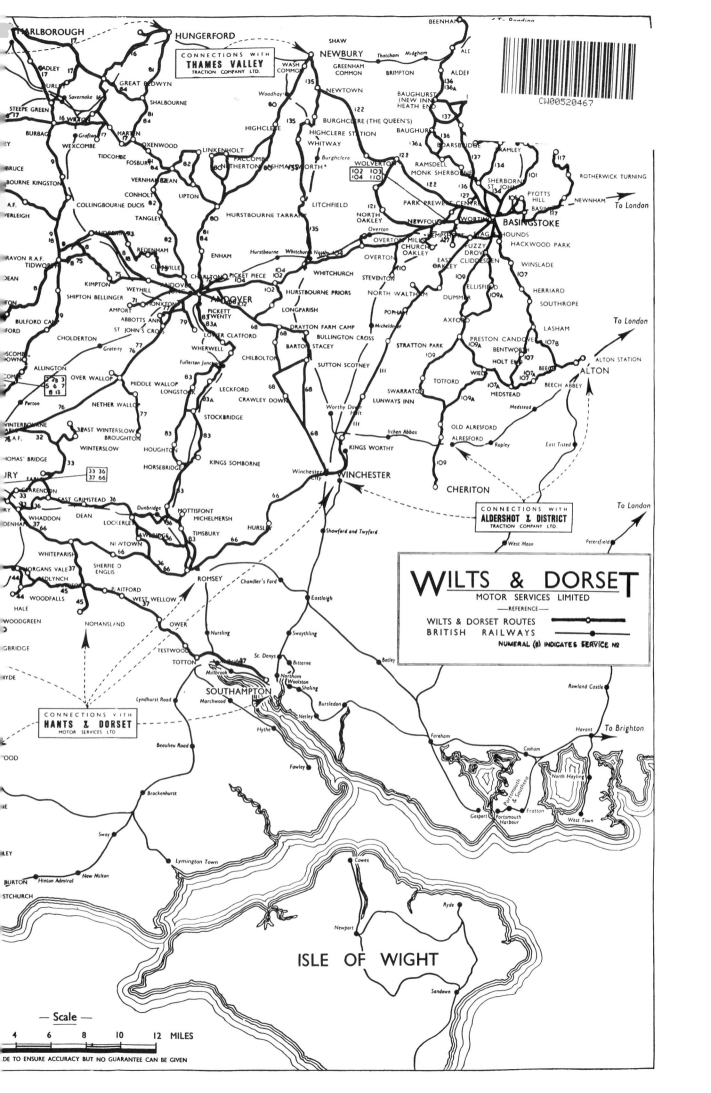

Wilts & Dorset

WILTS & DORSET

1915 - 1995

Eighty Years of Motor Services

Steve Chislett

to all employees of the Wilts & Dorset Bus Company,
past, present and future

WILTS & DORSE**T**
MOTOR SERVICES LIMITED

Week-end Leave Express Services

FOR

MILITARY AND R.A.F. PERSONNEL

FROM

Salisbury Plain Camps, Blandford Camp, Middle Wallop, etc., etc.

Our Representatives attend the above Camps every week for Advance Bookings to London and Other Important Places

---

LET US HELP YOU with All Your Travel Problems

First published 1995

Millstream Books
18 The Tyning
Bath BA2 6AL

This books has been set in 11 point Palatino
Printed in Great Britain by The Amadeus Press, Huddersfield

© Stephen M Chislett 1995

ISBN 0 948975 40 7

Details of the cover photographs can be found on pages 18, 60, 77 and 109

Contents

Introduction   6

Foreword   7

Chapter One: The Early Years   8

Chapter Two: Regulated Services   15

Chapter Three: Harvesting the Effects of War   30

Chapter Four: The Rising & Setting of the Silver Star   34

Chapter Five: Venture Forth to Nationalization and NBC   43

Chapter Six: A Return to Wilts & Dorset   87

Chapter Seven: Deregulation and Further Competition   96

Chapter Eight: Destination - The 21st Century   101

Appendix A: Fleetlist for 1965   122

Appendix B: Fleetlist for 1983   124

Appendix C: Fleetlist for 1995   125

CHARGES *for* DOGS
ACCOMPANYING FARE PAYING PASSENGERS

In accordance with the following scale:

	Adult Fare	Dog Fare	Adult Fare	Dog Fare
Salisbury City Services ⎫	1½d.	2d.	4d.	4d.
Andover Town Services ⎬	2d.	2d.	4½d.	5d.
Basingstoke Town ⎭	2½d.	3d.	5d.	5d.
Services	3d.	3d.	5½d.	6d.
	3½d.	4d.		
Other Services	Half Passenger Single Fare		... Minimum 6d.	

Please see front of book for full particulars, Regulations and Conditions, para. (17).

Introduction

Accurate histories of Wilts & Dorset Motor Services Ltd and Silver Star have been published in the past and this book, unlike these, is not intended to be a full history but rather it highlights aspects of the old and the new Wilts & Dorset companies together with businesses that have been absorbed. The years under National Bus Company control, when much of the time was spent operating under the Hants & Dorset fleetname, have been detailed in a number of books and are not covered here.

Deciding which photographs should be included has been a very difficult task. Wherever the photographer is known this is credited at the end of each caption and if there are any errors in this area I sincerely hope that those affected will accept my apologies. Every effort has been made to identify the rightful owners but many photographs have been supplied from collections without carrying any, or insufficient, detail to enable contact to be made.

A number of individuals have given great assistance in the production of this volume. Dave Elliott and Bill Cannings, both from Wilton, near Salisbury, supplied their photograph collections, as did Dave Withers of the Bristol Vintage Bus Group. Among others who helped was Lionel Tancock who supplied timetables from 1933, 1943 and the late 1940s and early 1950s, in addition to his personal collection of photographs.

Individuals who gave permission for their photographs to be reproduced are named in the credits to each caption but particular thanks must go to Mike Hodges of Whitstable; Martin Curtis of Bristol; Mike Walker of Cardiff; Brian Pike and Gerald Good of Salisbury; Peter Trevaskis of Guildford; and the collection of the Wilts & Dorset Bus Company.

Considerable help in compiling the captions was given by Chris Harris from Wilts & Dorset's head office in Poole and lengthy periods of reading and checking the manuscipt was undertaken by Chris Slark of Salisbury. Help from Jeremy Weller of Swanage and Mike Robins from the Company's head office is also acknowledged.

Although some of the above are employees of the Wilts & Dorset Bus Company, it must be emphasised that this is not an official publication of the Company, though it has benefited from material and guidance provided by the Company and its employees.

Once again my family has borne disruption and inconvenience during the compilation of this book and my thanks must be expressed to my wife Deirdre, sons Jeremy, Billy and Caleb, and daughters Mary and Anna for putting up with the chaos which often affected their lives.

My hope is that readers enjoy the contents of the book which may rekindle memories of the past or encourage hopes for the future. Whatever period of time particularly interests you, I trust that these pages will give pleasure. Comments and corrections will be gladly received through my puiblisher.

Steve Chislett
Salisbury, April 1995

Bibliography

The following books and publications were consulted during the compilation of this work:

The Fleet History of Wilts & Dorset Motor Services Ltd and Venture Ltd - published by The PSV Circle and Omnibus Society in March 1963

Buses Illustrated and *Buses*, various editions - published by Ian Allan Ltd

Varoius *Fleet Lists* published by Ian Allan Ltd

The Salisbury Times and other newspapers relevant to the 1930s

Company records, timetables and publicity

Foreword

Wilts & Dorset has had a long and proud tradition of public service to the community for 80 years.

Steve Chislett's story of the early days of formation, competition and acquisition draws a fascinating comparison with what has happened in the bus industry since deregulation and competition were reintroduced in 1986.

The struggles for route supremacy in the 20s, the court battles for licences under regulation in the 30s, and the huge stimulus provided by the Military Camps on Salisbury Plain are all described using documents of the time.

Deregulation in the 80s brought its own battles reminiscent of the 20s, but the challenge for the late 90s will be to fulfil the increasingly important role that public transport will play in our towns and cities.

While the achievements of the early pioneers are celebrated in this book, it is the experience they gained and the standards they set that will carry the Company forward into the next century.

Hugh Malone
Managing & Finance Director
Wilts & Dorset Bus Company

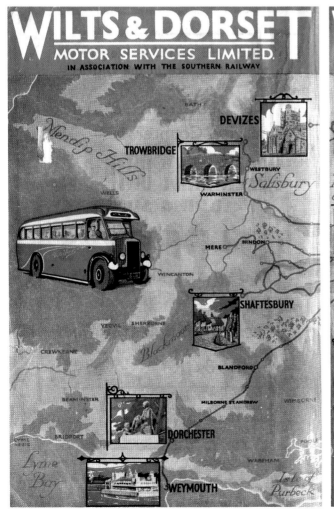

Cover of the Wilts & Dorset Motor Services timetable dated 6 June 1948 (L P Tancock collection)

Chapter One: The Early Years

The Company was registered on 31 December 1914 and commenced trading in February 1915 in the Salisbury area with one bus. Records show that no opportunities for business profits were expected to be overlooked and the Company was authorised to operate businesses of tramway, light railway, motor or other omnibus, carriage and van proprietors and, additionally, to act as a manufacturer and dealer in trams, etc. It can reasonably be assumed that the 'etc' mentioned in the Articles of Association for the Company when it was formed related to the construction and manufacture of bus chassis and bodies. The Wilts & Dorset name had been used by the Wilts & Dorset Banking Company Limited until it was taken over by Lloyds Bank in 1913 when the name disappeared. Disenchantment by local people at this decision resulted in the name being chosen for the new bus company operating between Amesbury and Salisbury from 1915. The plate of the old banking company can still be seen on the wall of Lloyds Bank in Blue Boar Row, Salisbury.

Initially, the Company's registered office was based at 46 High Street in Amesbury but from about February 1917 it was transferred to the offices of a Mr G H Davis at 2 St Thomas's Square in Salisbury. Mr Davis's income at the time was derived from acting as an auctioneer and estate agent. He had become a director of the Company in May 1915. The first secretary for the Company was Mr A D Mackenzie who had gained a good reputation through his working for the Southdown company, and the first shareholders involved with the Wilts & Dorset Company are listed as A E Cannon, who is recorded as a mechanical engineer and was another individual well-connected with Southdown, and an agriculturalist, P E Lephard. When G H Davis became a shareholder he was also joined by a Salisbury confectioner, Mr F Sutton. In June 1919, Davis became secretary for the Company by which time his shareholding had been increased from his original £5,500 stake to £10,000 in £1 shares.

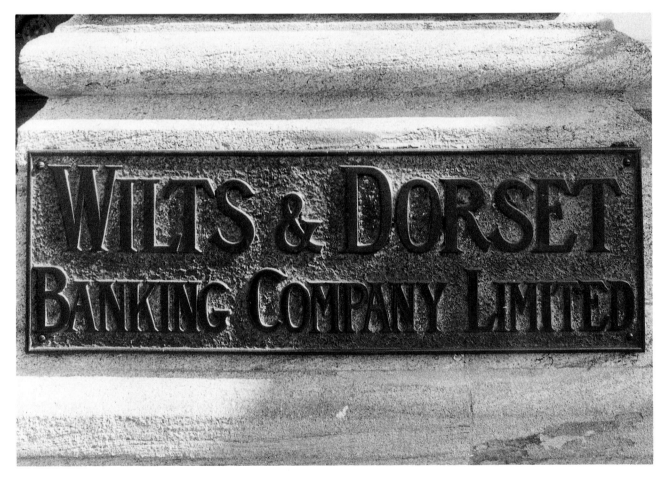

The original route between Salisbury and Amesbury was gradually expanded to cover services from Salisbury to West Hampshire and East Dorset in addition to a number of journeys within Wiltshire. In September 1919 Salisbury city services commenced, including a Salisbury to Wilton route, and the Company very much felt that they were the pioneers in supplying these areas with better standards of public transport.

According to a report in the *Salisbury Journal*, dated 7 June 1919, the Watch Committee recommended that the motor hackney licence sought by Wilts & Dorset Motor Services Company should be granted. It was stated, however, that should the Company operate journeys beyond the city boundary they would have to make their own arrangements with Wiltshire County Council regarding payment of the appropriate fees for use of the roads for which the county was responsible. Those present at the Watch Committee meeting thought that the service was going to be a great advantage to the city.

An article in *Modern Transport* dated 23 March 1929 included No 62 in a series called 'Organisation of Road Transport Services' on Wilts and Dorset Motor Services, Limited. In this account it was stated that total mileage amounted to 24,500 miles per week which rose during the summer months to 35,000.

"Although an area which attracts much visitor traffic the bulk of traffic carried was regular all-the-year-round services made up of market folk, workmen going to and from the camps, school children and troops, a special system of warrant ticket being in vogue for the last named. Many of the longer runs from Salisbury to Bournemouth, Andover, Marlborough, Shaftesbury and Southampton are very well patronised and particularly so in the summer months, besides which town services are operated to the extent of 8,500 miles per week, the headway varying between five and ten minutes, according to the volume of traffic to be carried. Garages were established at Bulford, Larkhill and Tidworth in the camp area and at Woodfalls, Marlborough, Broadchalke, Fordingbridge and Wilton."

Some fifty vehicles of AEC, Leyland and Dennis types were used and it was the intention to replace older vehicles with the Dennis 30 cwt vehicles for 18-seater work and Leyland Lions for 32- and 36-seaters. Additionally, the charabanc fleet consisted of eight 32-seaters, one 23-seater and one 18-seater for extensive excursion work at the time of the article. These were principally used for operating excursions to Stonehenge and Bournemouth and private hire work.

All vehicles at this time were fitted with pneumatic tyres of Dunlop manufacture and run on a mileage basis; one set of tyres averaged between 25,000 and 30,000 miles. Maintenance work was carried out in the rear of the main garage which had been divided off to form a workshop. Docking was carried out once a month and comprised attention to steering, brakes, clutches and minor adjustments to engines. When vehicles had completed between 40,000 and 50,000 miles a general overhaul was carried out. For this work to be carried out six mechanics and one bodymaker were employed and great use made of replacement parts supplied by the manufacturers. According to this report very little machine work was carried out on site with the only equipment being a couple of centre lathes, drilling machines and a grinder wheel. Examination of the bodywork was also made during the overhaul and any minor repairs carried out at the garage. Following completion of all necessary work the vehicles were taken to local coachbuilders to be painted and varnished.

Until June 1920 the Company had been a private company but from that date it became a public concern in which many local individuals took shares. At the time, the operation of bus services was seen as particularly lucrative and, consequently, attractive to investors when very few people possessed their own transport.

Certain services around the Salisbury area became subject to intense competition from other operators. The initial competition came from a company operating under the 'Victory' fleetname, managed by Mr E M Coombes. He received licences from the Salisbury Watch Committee to run buses between Salisbury and Wilton in 1920. The life of this company was particularly short-lived, having been bought by Wilts & Dorset for approximately £5,000 in 1921.

Expansion of routes as a normal commercial development continued with services from Salisbury to Southampton and Bournemouth, starting by early 1921. Two double-deckers had been purchased by Wilts & Dorset to operate the Wilton to Salisbury journeys against the competition from Salisbury and District Motor Services Ltd, often referred to as 'Yellow Victory'.

In May 1927 the Company increased the

number of buses on the Wilton route from four to six buses an hour just before the introduction of competitive journeys run by Sparrow and Vincent and operating under the Victory Motor Services name. The Mr Vincent involved with this company was the same man who had driven buses for the previous Victory Buses owned by E M Coombes.

The latter's application to the Watch Committee received "good sponsorship" from Alderman Lapham who was chairman of that committee and who put the application forward to the City Council at that meeting. It might well be supposed that Mr Lapham had some feeling of goodwill towards Sparrow and Vincent, particularly as they had been responsible for supplying transport for the annual outing of Mr Lapham's staff.

The following year, Sparrow and Vincent were granted further licences to operate journeys between Salisbury and West Harnham again in direct competition with services already offered by Wilts & Dorset. This situation was not unique to Salisbury and was being experienced in all areas of the country. As far as the Salisbury area was concerned the timetables were being changed so frequently that it led to particularly unsettled conditions and confusion for the public. Attempts by the Watch Committee to stabilise matters between the two operators by requesting both to run in accordance with the timetables agreed by the parties and the Chief Constable of the police met with limited success. Inevitably, Sparrow and Vincent would run in accordance with the timetable for the first few days and then resume their 'pirating' tactics of operating up to seven or eight minutes early or very much later than scheduled according to the position of Wilts & Dorset's buses at the time. The Directors of Wilts & Dorset kept the Watch Committee updated by letter of irregularities in Sparrow and Vincent's operations which eventually resulted in a number of these not even being acknowledged.

Despite this, the Company was always keen to accommodate requests from the City Council and in response to criticisms of overloading on certain journeys the Company ordered the latest type of covered top double-deckers in July 1929. The Directors hoped that this action again demonstrated their willingness and effort to assist the Council and the public in catering for peak loading demands. In addition the Company

diverted journeys to Devizes Road in response to a letter from the Chief Constable, but Sparrow and Vincent immediately began to take advantage of this, virtually abusing the concession made by the Company in this respect. The Company, quite obviously, made very strong representations about this totally unacceptable situation and were unhappy at the reply that each company was as bad as the other. When the Chief Constable was asked to substantiate this allegation he was, fortunately, unable to supply any evidence that the Wilts & Dorset journeys were being deliberately run off-schedule.

During late January 1930 the Traffic Manager of Wilts & Dorset was advised by the Chief Constable that the Company would be required to operate in accordance with timetables prepared by the police, this fact being confirmed by letter to the Company Secretary setting out the actual running times for certain buses. This had been done without any consultation and included departure times from points outside the borough such as Wilton, Stratford and Laverstock. A number of inaccuracies were found by the Directors in the Chief Constable's submission but a reply from the Chief Constable in February 1930 stated that "my Committee are determined to enforce good timekeeping to the full extent of their powers". Later in the month Sparrow and Vincent visited the Company's offices and stated that there seemed no doubt that both operators would have to comply with the Chief Constable's timetables from 1 April 1930.

A letter was received from Sparrow and Vincent a few days later offering their six buses for £12,000 and indicating that this would give Wilts & Dorset a monopoly "on the Town Services etc". The Directors, having previously bought out the Coombes' concern at a high price, declined the offer particularly as the purchase was no guarantee of a monopoly and there was no reason to suppose that another firm would not obtain licences to operate the same routes and then come along to be bought out and so on ad infinitum.

The previous tactics of Sparrow and Vincent recommenced and the Company Secretary wrote to the Chief Constable complaining of the opposition's continued bad practices and total disregard for complying with the timetable. The Chief Constable's reaction was totally unexpected when he decided that he would refuse to renew the licences for buses carrying registration numbers MW 3373, MW 4596, MW 4597, MW 6050, MW 6051, MW 6288 and MW 7048. In addition he restricted other vehicles so that five buses were licensed as Class A to run from Devizes Road to Market Place only with one bus to act as a spare, with 34 vehicles which were formerly Class A now licensed as Class B for use on country services only. It was a condition of all licences that the vehicles must run in accordance with the timetables approved by the committee. The Company, needless to say, appealed to the Ministry of Transport which was acknowledged by the Chief Constable on 12 July 1930 in a letter which also mentioned that the vehicle licences had been issued "in accordance with the timetables SUBMITTED to the Council" and not "APPROVED by the Committee". The Company's main point of appeal was the requirement for flexibility and the need for buses to be interchangeable from one route to another to maintain service provision on all routes as was covered in the Roads Act, 1920.

This whole matter was reported by the *Salisbury Times* in some detail but it was not until the implementation of the 1930 Road Traffic Act in 1931 that the problem was eventually resolved.

Commercial expansion also continued from time to time and included a route from Salisbury to Andover via Amesbury and Tidworth, starting in May 1927. The operation of this service resulted in Wilts & Dorset vehicles coming into contact with those operated by Venture Ltd, a Basingstoke-based operator. Venture was owned by Tom Thornycroft and had developed during the General Strike of 1926 as an addition to the family's chassis-manufacturing business. The bus-operating aspect was later taken over by Wilts & Dorset on 1 January 1951.

Further competition, this time because of Wilts & Dorset's decision, occurred in June 1930 when the Company decided to run between Andover and Newbury which for some ten years had been the sole province of L A Horne of Andover. Aggressive cuts in fares eventually resulted in Mr Horne withdrawing from stage carriage operations to concentrate on contract work.

A number of newspaper articles from the period give an idea of the intensity of the competitive environment. One such report appeared on 5 December 1930 and reads:

"On Monday 1 December a Conductor employed by Messrs Sparrow and Vincent was fined for causing an obstruction in Bridge Street on 20 November when his bus was stood by the County Hotel for nine minutes. It was seen to remain from 3.36pm to 3.45pm. Afterwards it returned and caused a similar obstruction for eight minutes. PC Larcombe stated that at 3.39pm a Wilts & Dorset double-deck bus drew in behind the blue bus and remained six minutes being unable to pull out."

Later that month on 18 December 1930 it is recorded that the Directors recognised the value of their workforce by issuing the following:

"As the Board of Directors are desirous of expressing their appreciation of the services rendered by all the Company's employees during the year 1930 the staff are asked to accept gratuities at the following rates:

One Year's Service or Over	£1
Under One Year	10/-
Boy Apprentices	At Half the Above Rates"

One of Wilts & Dorset's first buses was this 37-hp Scout with 33 seats, registered IB-804, which was purchased in March 1915. The body was built locally. It is photographed here outside Salisbury Guildhall. The bus was withdrawn in February 1917 having been used on the Company's first service between Amesbury and Salisbury via Woodford. (D A Elliott collection)

Received by Wilts & Dorset in June 1919, No 7 (CD 3330) was an AEC YC three-ton charabanc with a Harrington 31-seat body. Rebodied as a double-decker in 1921 it then carried a non-standard livery combining a red lower deck with a yellow and black top deck. Loaded to capacity it is seen in its charabanc days on a private hire. (Bill Cannings collection)

With the destination blind set for Wilton HR 1952 later obtained fleet number 22. It was a long-wheelbase Thornycroft J originally delivered to Salisbury & District Motor Services Ltd in 1920 and taken over by Wilts & Dorset in August 1921. It is seen equipped with an open-top 45-seat body with external staircase which was replaced with a Harrington body of similar design in 1923. This vehicle was withdrawn from the fleet in 1928 and the chassis sold to a farmer in Berkshire. (Bill Cannings collection)

Delivered in October 1923, Leyland G7 No 27 carried registration number HR 9541 and a Harrington 51-seat open-top body with external staircase. Seen here at Blue Boar Row, Salisbury on 25 June 1926, it is operating on the Service 2 route to Wilton. The bus was withdrawn in November 1933. (Pamlin Prints, Croydon)

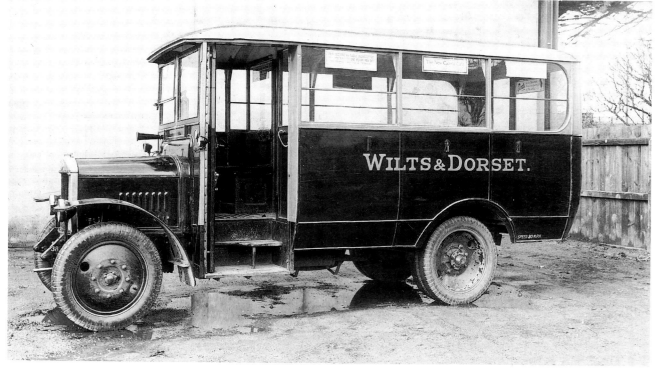

In 1927 Wilts & Dorset purchased a number of 19-seat Dennis 30-cwt vehicles including MR 8637 which was allocated fleet number 38. The body was by Short Brothers of Rochester and the bus entered service in February that year, only to be withdrawn just over four years later in May 1931 and sold to a motor business in Deptford, London. (Bill Cannings collection)

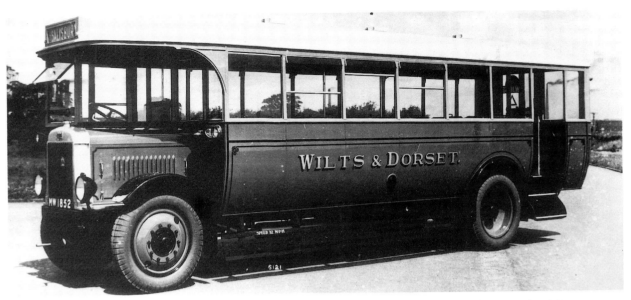

Received by Wilts & Dorset in May 1928 , Leyland PLSC3 No 56 (MW 1852) carried a 36-seat rear-entrance body. It was allocated Police Plates 100, 130 and 186 by Salisbury, Bournemouth and Southampton Police respectively. Rebodying by Beadle in June 1946 gave a 32-seat body featuring sliding windows and two-aperture destination indicators front and rear, the latter positioned below the window. It was withdrawn from service in July1950). (Bristol Vintage Bus Group - L P Tancock collection)

Staying in service with Wilts & Dorset until November 1952, No 66 (MW 4594) was new in June 1929. A Leyland TS1 with 32-seat rear-entrance Harrington coach body, it is seen in original form with canvas hood heading a line of Wilts & Dorset vehicles on a private hire in Newbridge Road, Salisbury. (Bill Cannings collection)

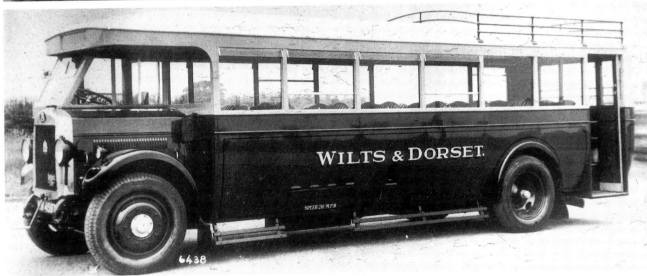

Leyland Lion LT1 (No 69), new in July 1929, carried a 31-seat rear-entrance body. It was withdrawn in November 1952, having been rebodied with a Beadle 32-seat body in 1947. (Bill Cannings collection)

Chapter Two: Regulated Services

All bus service operators were affected by the 1930 Road Traffic Act which transferred the responsibility for driver, conductor and service licensing from local authorities and police to Traffic Commissioners who were appointed by central government. Under these revised arrangements each operator would be required to apply for a registration for every stage carriage bus route, excursion or tour. Any variation required also had to be applied for and competitors or other interested parties were entitled to object to any proposals submitted for a variety of reasons, including abstraction of revenue from an established route through competition. This was, therefore, a complete reversal of the situation before the introduction of the 1930 Road Traffic Act when there had not been any real control over bus service provision. Applications, even though particularly sound, could be refused as a result of any number of objections.

Fares for each individual journey also required licensing and the income of any operator could be drastically affected if an application for a specific scale of fares was refused or amended.

At a meeting in Salisbury in July 1931 in the Guildhall, the Traffic Commissioners for the Southern Area outlined the principles of the revised arrangements and also heard a large number of applications for registration of bus services which included certain conflicting applications from rival companies. Under the new scheme matters were dealt with very much in line with courts of law and, in fact, the decision of the Traffic Commissioner was legally binding. Because of this the use of solicitors to fight the Company's corner was the normal practice until the 1985 Transport Act was implemented on 26 October 1986. A number of these solicitors became experts in dealing with hearings at Traffic Courts and some spent a great deal of time travelling the country to represent companies' interests.

One power of the Traffic Commissioners was to designate picking-up and stopping places and decide appropriate roads for service buses to use. This resulted, it was reported in the *Salisbury Times* on 3 July 1931, in the Commissioners not allowing the larger main-line buses seating 28 or 32 passengers to tackle the smaller roads and country lanes because it would not only be a danger to the public but in addition an interference with agriculture. During the transition period the Traffic Commissioners took a great deal of notice of the opinions of the Chief Constable and City Council, the previous "controllers of buses", when making decisions on whether or not to grant applications.

The first application to be dealt with was that submitted by Wilts & Dorset Motor Services to operate buses between Salisbury and Laverstock, Meyrick Avenue, Milton Road, West Harnham, Stratford Bridge, Devizes Road and Wilton. In each case Sparrow and Vincent were the objectors. It had been suggested by the Chairman of the Watch Committee that both parties should attempt to present some type of agreement at the hearing but this was not forthcoming. Following lengthy discussion and subject to certain conditions being attached to both operators' licences the applications were granted. A further 33 applications from Wilts & Dorset were for stage carriage services between Salisbury and Tidworth, Marlborough, Andover, Romsey, Bournemouth, Southampton, Woodfalls, Shaftesbury, Weymouth, Devizes, "etc". To add weight to the granting of the application for additional journeys on the Andover service it was said that the Company was able to supply the public with off-street waiting facilities. The extra journeys were required to meet the demands of soldiers and workmen travelling on the route. Between 1 January 1931 and July 1931 the number of journeys run had amounted to 388 per week which had during that period carried a total of 302,950 passengers. An example of the weekly numbers carried was given as 12,728 during the week ending 12 June 1931.

On the second day of the hearings Messrs Sparrow and Vincent applied for licences to run buses on routes between Laverstock and Ditchampton; Milton Road and Ditchampton; Devizes Road and Waters Road; Salisbury and Alderbury; and Station Road and the Race Course. The recorded objectors to these applications were the Town Clerks of Salisbury and Wilton, the Wilts & Dorset Bus Company and the Chief Constables of Wiltshire and Salisbury. The objections centred around the fact that the agreement reached the previous day would result in a decrease in the number of journeys whereas the applications on this particular day would result in an increase. The objection from the Chief Constable of Salisbury was withdrawn when the implications of the agreement were clarified and Sparrow and Vincent emphasised their wish not to interfere with the operation of the Wilts & Dorset journeys. Authorisation was also being sought to operate excursions and tours although not necessarily to compete with those requested by Wilts & Dorset from Salisbury and Andover. Some debate took place regarding what was felt to be a reasonable fare on some of the excursions and tours which would ensure that the advertised trip would run. The following is an extract of part of the discussion:

> The Chairman: If you only get ten people or five people, do you start?
> Witness: We put on a smaller coach.
> The Chairman: What is the minimum number with which you would start? Would you take two?
> Witness: We should not take two. We should probably arrange with one of our competitors to take the passengers.
> The Chairman: If there were no other competitors going to the same place would you run?
> Witness: Yes.
> Mr Privett: You can always fall back on the Southern Railway
> Mr E Gilbert Woodward (for the Southern Railway): At 5 shillings (laughter)

During the hearing concerning an application from W Rowland & Son of Castle Street, Salisbury to run tours and excursions to a large number of popular resorts, Mr Privett who had inspected the list asked "Heaven's Gate - where is that?" Mr Hiscock, representing Rowlands, replied "We are all hoping to find it some day" which resulted in laughter. Mr Privett, not to be outdone, added "It is not near Epsom, I suppose" to renewed laughter.

Various other applications were heard from J Connolly of Woodfalls; H Chant of Shrewton; E Grant of Winterslow; and from Lavington and Devizes Motor Services Limited.

As a result of the hearings the Company was informed that the applications had been granted except that the Company was allowed to run three trips an hour to Wilton with Sparrow and Vincent permitted two, and on the Devizes Road section

the Company was only allowed to run five trips an hour instead of six. These were effective from 2 September 1931.

Complaints continued to appear in the local newspapers regarding the congestion caused by buses and the difficulties being experienced by intending passengers waiting on the streets. The problems were as bad following the change of bus service control as they were before and the situation was labelled as "A Public Scandal" by the *Salisbury Times*. Hearings for a number of competitive services affecting Wilts & Dorset were heard during a four-day sitting by the Traffic Commissioners at Southampton. One of particular interest was that submitted by Messrs Shergold and White of Porton Camp, Salisbury who wished to run a service from Larkhill to Salisbury. This was objected to by Wilts & Dorset but the application was supported by Captain Learmont on behalf of Larkhill garrison who stated that the camp was entirely dependent upon buses. The Wilts & Dorset buses were, he said, unpunctual and very often people had to stand on the footboard outside the door. He added that there appeared to be no effort on the part of Wilts & Dorset to cater for the needs of the station. When asked by the Chairman whether if the Wilts & Dorset buses adhered to their timetable the service would be sufficient, Captain Learmont replied that it would. The case was adjourned for a month to see whether the Company was able to run the advertised service satisfactorily. As far as the Commissioners were concerned the best detectives in these matters were the public themselves who should report the facts to them and if it was felt appropriate licences would be revoked. In 1932 there continued to be complaints about too many buses being run by competing companies within Salisbury and a number of applications were made by other operators within the Company's area, one of which, in October 1932, resulted in the Traffic Commissioner remarking that they were at a loss to understand why there should be so much trouble in this small area - referring to applications for the Woodfalls and Redlynch communities together with those around Hamptworth and Plaitford. If all the operators were to work together, he said, all the trouble would come to an end. Throughout the early 1930s applications and counter proposals were lodged with the Traffic Commissioners leading to great expense being incurred by the Company in presenting its own plans and objecting to those from other operators which would affect the revenue base of Wilts & Dorset. Complications abounded at the hearings, causing the decision-making process for the Traffic Commissioners to be more than a little difficult at times.

Joint applications were now submitted by the Company together with Hants & Dorset Motor Services including a plan to run between Salisbury and Winchester which was refused in favour of an alteration to the licences held by Mr R Chisnell trading as King Alfred from Winchester. Such was the feeling from certain quarters about the restrictive practices imposed by the new legislation that some held a meeting at the Red Lion Hotel in Salisbury demanding that the Minister of Transport abolish the Southern Traffic Area, eventually pursuing the request to the House of Lords.

On 1 December 1933 it was announced in the *Salisbury Times* that Wilts & Dorset was to take over the Sparrow and Vincent business of Victory and it was emphasised that the amalgamation would produce a number of benefits for the travelling public and other residents alike. The takeover became effective before the end of the year. In an article published in the *Salisbury Times* in March 1934 the Company stated that the number of passengers travelling on country services was close on three million per year.

A major improvement, as far as Salisbury was concerned, was the completion of Salisbury Bus Station between Endless Street and Rollestone Street in August 1939. At the same time the Company moved its offices from their previous location in St Thomas's Square onto the upper floor of the new building.

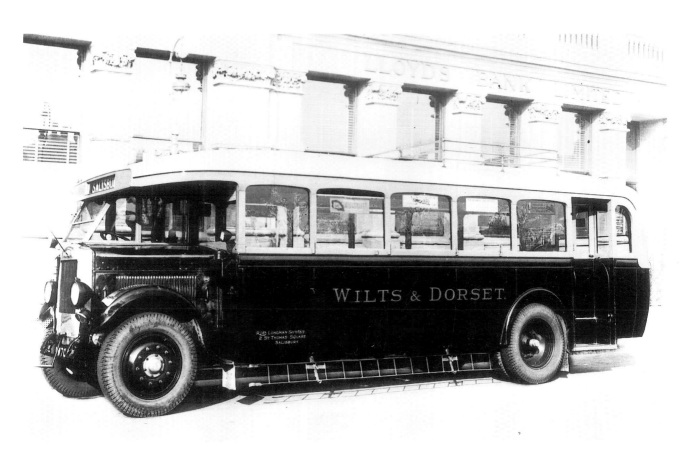

A full stop appears on the fleetname on Leyland Lion LT2 No 92 (MW 7053) with Leyland 35-seat rear-entrance bodywork. New in July 1930, the vehicle lasted until September 1953. Seen here at Blue Boar Row, Salisbury the vehicle's legal lettering carries the long-serving name of R I H Longman as Secretary with 2 St. Thomas' Square, Salisbury as the legal address. This makes the photograph a pre-August 1939 view. (Bill Cannings collection)

A brace of petrol-engined Morris Commercial Viceroy vehicles arrived in May 1932 equipped with Harrington 20-seat coach-style bodies. One was No 127 (WV 652), seen above at Amesbury Bus Station in 1934. Note the ornate fleetname style and luggage container on the roof typical of the period. Withdrawn in July 1941 it was then allocated to the Air Ministry in London. (Bill Cannings collection)

Another view of No 127 comes from a postcard bearing the crest of the Royal Studio, Salisbury. This clearly shows the elegant curtains provided for the passengers' comfort. (Bill Cannings collection)

Local coachbuilder Heaver of Durrington supplied 24-seat front-entrance bodies for six Morris Commercial Viceroy buses in April and May 1931. One of these is seen illustrating the position and style of the front entrance which allowed one-man-operation with these vehicles at a later date. Note the style of fleetname on this broadside view. These buses remained with Wilts & Dorset until withdrawal between December 1940 and May 1943. (Bill Cannings collection)

New in July 1934, No 117 (WV 5526) was one of a pair of Leyland Tiger TS6 vehicles received complete with 32-seat Harrington coach-style bodies. This was rebuilt by Portsmouth Aviation in October 1946 and withdrawn in April 1953. It is seen here in the 1930s at Newbridge Road, Salisbury. (D A Elliott collection)

Five Leyland TD1 buses with Leyland 48-seat bodywork were received by Wilts & Dorset in February 1931 with two being delivered later in June that year. One was No 97 (MW 8754) seen here in Blue Boar Row, Salisbury in 1937 with Coronation decorations in the background. Note the 'piano front' style bodywork. (Bill Cannings collection)

This view is an earlier photograph of the same bus operating the St Mark's Church to Wilton (Ditchampton) service. The crew pose proudly with their vehicle which clearly demonstrates the 'piano front' style of bodywork. It was rebuilt by Eastern Coach Works in October 1944, retaining its 48-seat lowbridge capacity and remained in service until October 1951. (Bill Cannings collection)

A Leyland TD1, seen here as rebuilt by Eastern Coach Works in December 1945, is No 103 (MW 9397). When new in July 1931 the bus had a Leyland 48-seat lowbridge body. ECW fitted sliding windows, a new radiator and modified destination display. The bus is parked outside Castle Street Garage in Salisbury with the upper-deck grab rails clearly visible through the windows. It was withdrawn in July 1951. (Bill Cannings collection)

Lowbridge bodywork on double-deck buses was required in the Salisbury area due to the predominance of low rail bridges. In 1938 and 1939 seven Leyland TD5 vehicles carrying Park Royal 52-seat lowbridge bodies were received, all being withdrawn from service during 1956. One was No 163 (BHR 741) pictured here when new, in Newbridge Road. It was later rebuilt by the Company in November 1946. (Bill Cannings collection)

Leyland PLSC3 carrying registration number MW 2955 was new to Sparrow and Vincent in October 1928 and was purchased with that business by Wilts & Dorset in December 1933. It originally had a Leyland 36-seat body but is seen here looking resplendent with Salisbury Cathedral in the background and with a replacement Beadle 32-seat body fitted in November 1945. The vehicle left the fleet in July 1950. (Bill Cannings collection)

No 111 (WV 2381) in the fleet was new in January 1933. A Leyland TD2, it was originally supplied with a Leyland 48-seat lowbridge body. Here it is pictured on 3 January 1954 after having received an Eastern Coach Works 51-seat lowbridge body in September 1946. The bus was withdrawn in August 1954 only eight months after this photograph was taken. The chassis was later used as a lorry. (David J N Pennels - Bill Cannings collection)

Road conditions near Wilton Market Place look appalling as No 141 (WV 7475) passes over the temporary road surface. A Leyland Titan TD4 delivered in July 1935, it survived until February 1957, originally with a Leyland 52-seat body which was replaced by the Willowbrook body seen here in 1947, to be used later by Esso at their refinery in Fawley. (Bill Cannings collection)

Overleaf: Vehicles 144 (AHR 399) and 145 (AHR 400) were both Leyland Titan TD4 chassis fitted with two of the earliest examples of Leyland's metal-framed bodies. Received in July 1936 they were rebuilt by Wilts & Dorset in April 1948 and continued in service until February 1957 and March 1957 respectively. No 144 is seen leaving Amesbury Bus Station on Service 3 on 27 September 1953 and No 145 is at Blue Boar Row, Salisbury on Service 62 to St Mark's Church on 13 March 1957. In 1949 No 145 was fitted with experimental fluorescent lighting and was one of the first such installations of its kind, although this equipment was subsequently removed. (Both David J N Pennels - Bill Cannings collection)

Carrying the revised destination layout fitted in February 1953 is Bristol K5G No 198 (CHR 497) with Eastern Coach Works 52-seat lowbridge body. Seen here at Salisbury Bus Station, it was taken out of service in August 1959. Paper or painted advertisements, rather than the current vinyl displays, were the accepted method of bus advertising in those days. (D A Elliott collection)

New in 1931, this ex-Southdown Leyland TD1, No 25 (UF 7079) was received by Wilts & Dorset in June 1939 when it carried a Short Brothers 48-seat highbridge body. This was replaced by this Park Royal 50-seat lowbridge body in August 1941. It remained in service until October 1953 and is seen operating on Service 61 to Waters Road earlier that year on 7 January. It is interesting to compare its livery with the wartime drab of No 27 on page 31. (David J N Pennels - Bill Cannings collection)

Photographed in its rebodied state is No 252 (UF 7423) at Salisbury Bus Station, a Leyland TD1 with Duple 55-seat lowbridge bodywork which had been fitted in September 1942 and modified by Wilts & Dorset in November 1948. Having been new to Southdown in 1931, the bus completed 24 years in service, being withdrawn in January 1955. (Bill Cannings collection)

Daimler No 261 (CWV 779) turns out of New Canal into High Street, Salisbury en-route to Wilton on Service 60 during the mid-1950s. (D A Elliott collection)

Still wearing Wilts & Dorset livery and fleetnames but heading for Towyn on the North Wales coastline is Leyland TD1 MW 7051, formerly Wilts & Dorset No 90. New in 1930, it latterly carried an Eastern Coach Works body seating 51 passengers dating from 1946. It was sold to Crosville Motor Services in April 1952, becoming their No MG 645 before being withdrawn in August 1953. (R F Mack - L P Tancock collection)

Dating from February 1931, No 95 (MW 8752) was a Leyland Titan TD1 originally fitted with a Leyland 6.8 litre petrol engine and a Leyland 48-seat double-deck rear-entrance body. It later received a Leyland four cylinder 5.1 litre petrol engine only to be replaced yet again in December 1935 by a Leyland six-cylinder 8.6 litre diesel engine. The original body was rebuilt by Wilts & Dorset in March 1943 and again by Lancashire Aircraft in September 1946. No 95 was hired to Crosville Motor Services Ltd from August 1951 to April 1952 when it was transferred to the Crosville fleet until withdrawal in August 1953. (Bristol Vintage Bus Group - L P Tancock collection)

The bodywork readily indentifies Nottingham City Transport origins on 464 (TV 4958), which came to Wilts & Dorset in December 1944 with 11 other AEC Regents. Built in 1931, it carried a Brush 52-seat rear entrance highbridge body. During 1945-6 all these vehicles were reconditioned, increasing their capacity to 56 seats. It is seen at Basingstoke Garage shortly before withdrawal in 1953. (L P Tancock collection)

Only six new vehicles were delivered to Wilts & Dorset in 1933, including No 110 (WV 2380), one of six

Leyland TD2 double-deckers equipped with Leyland 48-seat bodies. The original six-cylinder 7.6 litre engine was replaced by an 8.6 litre diesel in March 1938 and a Gardner 5LW diesel unit later that year. March 1946 saw a replacement Willowbrook 51-seat lowbridge body carrying three-aperture destination displays at the front and rear, and sliding window ventilators. Seen here at Marlborough, it was withdrawn in August 1954 and sold to a Southsea showman a month later. (R F Mack - L P Tancock collection)

Chapter Three: Harvesting the Effects of War

Development of Wilts & Dorset was greatly influenced by the Second World War and the years immediately preceding the span of hostilities between 1939 and 1945. A massive influx of armed forces into the Salisbury Plain garrisons in the period leading up to the war resulted in extreme pressure being placed on the services operating to these camps and the areas around them.

To prepare the extra accommodation space for the troops who would be stationed on the plain, a large workforce required daily transport from the Salisbury district to the various camps, particularly around the Bulford and Larkhill areas. There was little time available to complete the barracks for the army conscripts and an emergency building programme was devised in order to achieve this under a veil of secrecy.

Such was the level of secrecy that the Company was only notified the day before that they would be expected to supply workers' buses from 0600 on the initial morning. At first only a few single-deckers were required to carry workers from Salisbury, Wimborne and Dorchester to Blandford Camp but the number of vehicles needed for this contract and the many others soon exceeded all expectations. Buses were hastily obtained from a number of operators all over the country including Hants & Dorset, Southdown, Tyneside, Brighton Hove and District, Eastern National, Maidstone and District together with its subsidiary company Chatham and District, as well as vehicles from Corporations in Nottingham, Birkenhead, Bolton and Huddersfield.

The contract for transport to Blandford Camp alone eventually needed 119 buses per day, this number almost equal to the number of buses used to provide all other services in the Company's area before the war. Development of air bases and 'shadow' factories resulted in additional contract work being given to Wilts & Dorset. Because of the urgency to press the extra buses into service immediately to cope with the demands from the War Department the vast majority of vehicles were operated in their original owners' liveries with many still carrying the destination blinds which they arrived with. The largest number of buses supplied by any one operator was 58 from Southdown Motor Services. A proportion of the double-deck arrivals were of highbridge layout

which restricted the possibilities of their use in a previously lowbridge-style fleet.

Maintaining the expanded fleet at the main workshops in Castle Street, Salisbury proved to be difficult but the standards required by the Ministry of Transport were met despite part of the Castle Street premises being commandeered for aircraft production. The Company, despite all the pressures it was then under, was able to start rebodying a number of the highbridge double-deckers that it had inherited to the lowbridge design which would allow the Company greater flexibility when using the vehicles. The rebuilding programme was so effective that many of the buses which were anticipated to have only a very short working life with the Company were able to continue in revenue-earning service well beyond the end of the war and frequently with other bus companies. Additional buses were loaned to the Company by London Transport between 1942 and 1944 to alleviate the demands being placed upon the Company's available passenger capacity particularly to War Department sites.

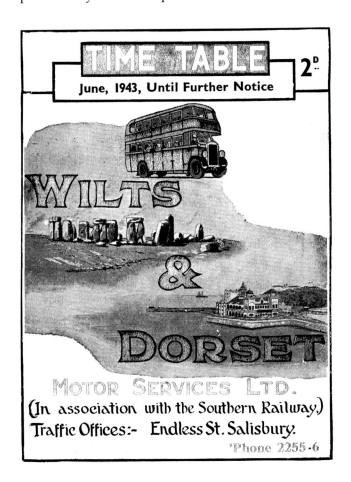

Among the first Bristol vehicles bought by Wilts & Dorset was No 195 (CHR 494) a Bristol K5G with 52-seat Eastern Coach Works lowbridge body. New in January 1940 it is pictured carrying Second World War 'black-out' white markings and headlamp masks. This bus remained in service with Wilts & Dorset until September 1959 and was later used by Esso at their oil refinery in Fawley. (Bristol Vintage Bus Group)

The added risk with bus operation during wartime was possible loss or damage caused by enemy action. No 68 (MW 4596) was damaged in July 1942 by a fire bomb when in Trowbridge. It is seen after being rebuilt by Eastern Coach Works in February 1943. Delivered in July 1927 it was withdrawn in November 1952. (Bill Cannings collection)

Acquired from Southdown in June 1939, UF 7396 was given fleet number 27. New in 1931, the Leyland TD1 first carried a Short Brothers 50-seat highbridge body, later replaced by a Brush lowbridge body seating 55, in March 1944. Pictured with its lowbridge body, it is wearing wartime livery and markings. (Bill Cannings collection)

Exterior and interior views of Castle Street Garage premises in Salisbury. Note the condition of the yard surface in this photograph taken during late 1945 and the full bicycle rack.

In the open yard view can be seen No 89 (MW 7050), a 1930 Leyland TD1 with Leyland 48-seat lowbridge body received in July that year, which was later rebuilt by Wilts & Dorset. Other vehicles here include No 32 (UF 7427), a 1931 Leyland TD1 with Short Brothers 50-seat highbridge body purchased by Wilts & Dorset from Southdown in June 1939, rebuilt as seen in January 1944 by Brush to 55-seat lowbridge layout. Displaying 'Salisbury 4' destination is No 244 (UF 7382) which began life as a similar vehicle to No 31 but was rebodied by Northern Coachbuilders with a 53-seat lowbridge body in June 1944. Single-deck No 184 (CHR 483), immediately behind this vehicle, is seen in original condition and is a Leyland Tiger TS8 carrying Harrington dual-purpose 32-seat rear-entrance bodywork, new in December 1939.

The interior view, taken after January 1947, shows among the occupants an unidentified Leyland Tiger TS8 alongside No 141 (WV 7475), a Leyland TD4 with revised bodywork and destination display by Willowbrook; an unidentified Leyland; and No 109 (WV 2379) a Leyland TD2, new in January 1933 which by this time had been rebodied by Willowbrook with a 51-seat lowbridge body. (both Bill Cannings collection)

Arriving in November 1929, Leyland LT1 No 73 (MW 5802) carried a 31-seat rear-entrance body. During 1939 it was converted into an ambulance together with Nos 71 and 72 of similar manufacture. In December 1945 it was rebodied, increasing the seats to 32, and incorporating a single-aperture destination indicator at the top of the window immediately in front of the rear entrance. It was withdrawn in June 1953. (L P Tancock collection)

Vehicle No 100 (MW 8757) arrived in May 1931 and is seen here at Winchester Bus Station. A Leyland TS1 with Harrington 32-seat coach bodywork and rear entrance, it remained in the fleet until January 1952, having been rebodied by Eastern Coach Works in June 1944. It was fitted with a Leyland six-cylinder 6.8 litre petrol engine. (L P Tancock collection)

Delivered as fleet number 193 (CHR 492) in January 1940, this Bristol K5G with Eastern Coach Works 52-seat lowbridge body is seen in Salisbury Bus Station carrying its original destination equipment. Note the advertisement extolling 'War Office' approval. The destination display was modified in September 1952 and the vehicle withdrawn in October 1958. (Bristol Vintage Bus Group)

Chapter Four: The Rising & Setting of the Silver Star

Of all competitive operators, Silver Star of Porton Down was the largest and potentially most dangerous opposition in the heart of Wilts & Dorset country until deregulation in 1986. Silver Star was recognised both locally and further afield as being a well-presented and professionally run public service operator during its lifespan between 1923 and 1963. This company should not be confused with another business called Tidworth Silver Star which made a short appearance in the early 1990s when it attempted to compete with Wilts & Dorset on a number of Salisbury City Services, particularly to the large Bemerton Heath housing estate on the western outskirts of the city.

The Silver Star business was formed in September 1923 after purchasing a Ford Model T chassis which was equipped with a canvas-hooded 14-seat body, supplied and built by Pitt of Fordingbridge and finished with polished aluminium panels. Registered HR 9447, it commenced operating a regular service between Allington, the company's original base, and Porton Camps through Winterbourne Gunner, Winterbourne Dauntsey and Winterbourne Earls to Salisbury. A reduced number of journeys were offered on Sundays on the route.

Various reasons have been suggested for the fleetname Silver Star being selected. One is that it appealed to the owners due to a popular waltz, although it has also been suggested that it may be partly because of Mr Shergold, one of the owners, having served some time on the destroyer *Morning Star*. Another is that it was due to the shining aluminium panels of their original vehicle.

The largest competitor for Silver Star was, obviously, Wilts & Dorset Motor Services Ltd who had been running routes around the Salisbury area since 1915 and had steadily grown in size and strength since that time. Other smaller operators, however, had already been supplying journeys in the areas now being served by Silver Star, particularly on Salisbury Market Days. In 1923 a regular service through the Bourne Valley was started between Salisbury and Tidworth via The Winterbournes (Earls, Dauntsey and Gunner) and Allington. This new facility offered three return journeys daily except on Sundays when this was reduced to two.

Expansion of the business continued slowly but it was the Second World War that would provide Silver Star with a substantial increase in work and revenue. During this period the company's base was moved from Allington to Porton Camp. By 1927 the fleet had increased to five vehicles including a Rolls Royce Silver Ghost chassis registered X 2500. This was converted into a six-wheeler by the owners themselves and later received a 20-seat coach body built by Wray's in south-west London. The proprietors, E W 'Eddie' Shergold and B F 'Ben' White, were so impressed with the qualities offered by the Rolls Royce that they decided to purchase a further example for conversion which was registered XY 8727.

As already mentioned in a previous chapter, the implementation of the Road Traffic Act of 1930 resulted in operators having to apply for registration of the services that they operated and Silver Star accordingly did so. Applications sought by the company included daily stage carriage services between Allington and Salisbury via Porton Camp; Salisbury and Andover via Amesbury, Bulford Camp, Tidworth and Ludgershall; Salisbury and Bulford Camp (Sling); together with numerous tours and excursions from both Salisbury and Porton Camp. All applications sought were granted by the Southern Area Traffic Commissioners except the one requested for a Salisbury to Andover service which was refused on the grounds that the Silver Star operation on the route was not sufficiently long-standing to warrant the licence being granted. Another slight problem was that, although the whole of the application for tours and excursions from Porton Camp had been granted, the request to run similar tours and excursions from Salisbury had been refused.

The refusal of the Salisbury to Andover application was particularly disappointing for the proprietors as a vehicle had been purchased especially to operate this route and had been completed with lettering advertising the service. A Leyland TS1, registered MW 8982, it had been sign-written with the words "Salisbury,

Amesbury, Bulford Camp, Tidworth, Andover".

Other work was soon available which was partly to compensate Silver Star for the lack of success in their endeavours to expand the stage carriage network of services further afield. Reasonable income was to come from carrying military bands from Salisbury Plain camps to various functions across the country. Although these were not exclusively operated by Silver Star the company obtained a good proportion of the available work.

Vehicles were being purchased when needed and included new and used examples throughout the history of the company. In the late 1920s and early 1930s these included AECs and Leylands, in particular a Leyland Lioness bus registered TR 2460 from Southampton Corporation which had been built in 1926.

During the period immediately preceding the Second World War substantial increases were experienced in the numbers of passengers using Silver Star's stage carriage services. This was particularly the case with travel to and from Winterbourne Dauntsey where construction of Figsbury Barracks was progressing urgently. In order to overcome the severe loading difficulties that this work produced, the company looked at providing additional capacity without increasing costs. They arrived at the same solution as Wilts & Dorset and purchased their first double-deckers. These materialised as six Leyland Titan TD1 lowbridge-bodied examples from Yorkshire Woollen District registered HD 4153- 4158 with 51 seats each.

Changes in the fleet owned by Shergold and White continued following the outbreak of hostilities particularly when the War Department requisitioned a number of their single-deck vehicles. Another was lost following an 'argument' with a tank at Targetts Corner, Porton in 1942 which, needless to say, the bus lost. The demands for travel and the non-availability of new vehicles because of the war effort resulted in a number of unusual makes of vehicle being obtained during and after the war including Tilling Stevens and Thornycrofts.

The effects of wartime had resulted in the Silver Star fleet suffering quite badly due, in some cases, to vehicles being well beyond their life expectancy or the effects of particularly arduous working on heavily-laden runs. New stock was to arrive, however, during 1947. In the January an all Leyland double-deck vehicle arrived in the shape of EAM 776, a PD1 carrying a 53-seat lowbridge body. During September, Leyland Tiger PS1/1 registered EMW 703 was received. Carrying a Duple 33-seat coach-style body this was to be the last new vehicle delivered to Silver Star with unpainted polished panelling which had been the hallmark of the fleet before the war.

Changes in the composition of the fleet continued from 1949 when a number of Leyland Titan TD4c double-deckers were bought from Birmingham City Transport carrying Leyland highbridge bodies which were later upseated from a capacity of 52 to 55 seats by the company. New buses were also received when in January 1951 an all Leyland PD2/1 arrived, carrying registration mark GWV 360 and a 56-seat lowbridge body.

Weekend leave express services for the military formed a major part of the company's income during the 1950s. These operated from the various camps on Salisbury Plain to almost every part of England. From 1947, due to the continued fuel rationing, Wilts & Dorset were providing a 'railhead' system of journeys from the camps to railway stations at either Salisbury or Andover Junction to enable connections with trains to London Waterloo and other destinations to be made. By 1950 Wilts & Dorset had been authorised to run additional feeder services to destinations further afield such as Bristol to connect with trains for South Wales; Portsmouth for trains to the South East; and Cheltenham or Oxford for trains to the Midlands and North.

Applications by a number of operators interested in running express services to cater for forces personnel were continually refused by the Traffic Commissioners following objections lodged by Wilts & Dorset and the Railway Executive who felt that the railhead facilities currently available were quite adequate. It was a surprise, therefore, for Silver Star to learn that Wilts & Dorset had been granted a licence to run a Boscombe Down to London express service in 1951. Following the granting of this licence, forces express services developed rapidly from the Salisbury Plain camps to London destinations run by a variety of local coach operators. These were later expanded to other destinations such as Birmingham, Preston, Liverpool, Leeds and Wales and included journeys run by both Silver Star and Wilts & Dorset. The camps at Bulford were considered to be the province of Silver Star, that at Boscombe Down to be Wilts & Dorset's, and those in other areas the province of other smaller operators.

These restrictions were not particularly acceptable to Silver Star who decided to expand their territory by running to Edinburgh, Glasgow and Newcastle upon Tyne against some fierce opposition from other operators involved in the supply of forces leave transport. By 1957, the operation of the forces leave express services had reached their peak with journeys usually departing camps on Salisbury Plain on Friday afternoons and returning from the various destinations on Sundays. The arrangement was that between eight and ten coaches would collect personnel from the camps to connect at Tidworth to exchange passengers onto the appropriate vehicles for the destinations required.

In addition to the express runs and local stage carriage journeys Silver Star continued its tours and excursions programme but, despite continual applications to the Traffic Commissioners, were not granted a licence to run any tours or excursions from Salisbury itself.

One-man operation of certain bus journeys was being introduced by Wilts & Dorset in 1955 on particularly poorly patronised journeys and this option was examined by Silver Star in some detail. Their first vehicle for this type of operation was purchased in August 1957 and arrived as PHR 829, a Leyland Tiger Cub carrying Harrington bodywork, seating 41 passengers with front entrance ahead of the front axle. This was the first of a batch of three similar vehicles which could be used on stage carriage or express work. Additional one-man operation was introduced in February 1958 when the two other vehicles were delivered with registrations PMW 386 and RAM 620.

The owners of Silver Star had a definite pride in their business which they attempted to demonstrate in the way that their vehicles were presented to the public. It was a great day for them in June 1959 when an early production model of the revolutionary Leyland Atlantean double-deck bus was delivered. This was the first rear-engined double-decker in the Salisbury area and carried a 73-seat lowbridge body built by Weymann with registration mark TMW 853. Because of the complete change in design the bus created much interest both locally and nationally.

Rivalry, thwarted by the effects of the 1930 Road Traffic Act, was still evident and Silver Star

wished to expand its stage carriage operations. In 1957 they applied to the Traffic Commissioners to operate an express service between Bemerton Heath on the west side of Salisbury to Porton Down Camp. As the proposal would take traffic from Wilts & Dorset and British Railways, both parties objected to the application but despite this the licence was granted.

From June 1959 a joint service between Salisbury and Swindon was introduced by Bristol Omnibus Company and Wilts & Dorset in spite of an objection from Silver Star. This decision, no doubt, led to the coordinated timetable being agreed between all three parties for the route along the Bourne Valley which provided a more even headway on the timetable on which Silver Star remained the major operator.

Further new Leyland Atlanteans arrived with VAM 944 in July 1960, XMW 706 in July 1961 and 1013 MW in March 1962. The company made a special application to the Traffic Commissioners in August 1960 to use these vehicles on their express services. The Commissioners conceded that the vehicles were considered to be suitable for operation on these routes but expressed concerns over the possibility that the vehicles might not strictly adhere to the designated scheduled roads. Not to be put off by this refusal, the company reapplied to run Atlanteans on express journeys to Liverpool via Birmingham and Manchester and also to Swansea. A Public Sitting was held by the Traffic Commissioners in Salisbury and Atlantean VAM 944 was parked in the Guildhall Square, outside the venue for the hearing. This hearing was not completed on the day and was later resumed in Bristol where the Traffic Commissioners announced that they were not satisfied with the arguments put forward by Silver Star and, therefore, refused the application.

This was an extremely bitter pill for Shergold to swallow as he had hoped to demonstrate Silver Star's lead in the field of express operation with appropriate double-deck vehicles and, obviously, benefit from being the pioneer of this in the Salisbury area. The third Atlantean, XMW 706, was being built at the time of the hearing and was to be completed with 61 luxury-style seats in the lowheight body and a Leyland 0.680 engine rather than the previous 0.600 units. The whole idea of using this vehicle on express services was now completely shattered through the decision of the Traffic Commissioners and the ordering of this vehicle proved to be a costly mistake as it never managed to realise its full earning potential associated with high-mileage express duties and relied on private hire and tours or excursions to earn its keep.

The last vehicle purchased by Silver Star was the fourth Leyland Atlantean registered 1013 MW which carried a 73-seat Weymann lowheight double-deck body and was equipped with a Leyland 0.680 engine.

In October 1962 Eddie Shergold died after having steered the company through many triumphs and problems since its formation. It was not long before the fate of the company was announced by Ben White when he revealed that the business was to be taken over by Wilts & Dorset Motor Services on the night of 4/5 June 1963. The journeys previously run by Silver Star would be operated by Wilts & Dorset from the start of service on Wednesday 5 June. The staff working for Silver Star were informed of this decision a week before

the news was made public. A number chose to join Wilts & Dorset at the change of ownership. The last Silver Star journey of all was the 2235 hours Salisbury to Porton Down journey via Idmiston operated by a Leyland PSUC1/2 carrying a Harrington 41-seat dual-purpose body.

Disposal of the former Silver Star vehicles resulted in the fleet being transferred to Wilts & Dorset with the exception of a number which went to Western National (six Leyland PSUs and one Commer TS3), Bristol Omnibus Company (three Leyland Atlanteans and one Trojan 13-seat minibus which was allocated to the 'Pump Room Special' service at Bath) and Super Coaches of Upminster (one Leyland PDR1/1, one Leyland RT7 and one Leyland PD2/1).

The silver and red livery and prominent silver star emblem displayed on the vehicles disappeared with great speed with those vehicles retained by Wilts & Dorset quickly receiving the new owner's livery and fleetnames.

Built in 1936, this Leyland Tiger TS7 had a half-cab Burlingham body. No 23 (AAM 756) was rebuilt by Heaver in 1952 with the full-fronted design shown when the vehicle was parked at Salt Lane Car Park in Salisbury. The vehicle, with others, was requisitioned for war work in 1939 but was the only one to be returned to Silver Star after the war. Note the Austin Ruby in the background. (D A Elliott collection)

The first post-war coach delivered to Silver Star was No 24 (EMW 703), a Leyland Tiger PS1/1 completed with a Duple 33-seat body in 1947. Seen parked among what would now be termed museum-piece transport, including a Wolseley, Ford, Rover and Austin, it did not transfer to Wilts & Dorset ownership. (D A Elliott collection)

Despite being built in 1937, Silver Star No 19 (COX 966) looks immaculate at Blue Boar Row, Salisbury complete with offside destination indicator in use and straight staircase. Purchased from Birmingham City Transport in January 1949, the highbridge body on this Leyland TD4c was upseated by Silver Star from the original capacity of 52 to 55. This bus overturned at Boscombe in 1952 but returned to work after being repaired by local coachbuilders Heaver. (D A Elliott collection)

Chipper Lane in central Salisbury is the location for Silver Star No 15 (HD 4155), an ex-Yorkshire Woollen District Leyland TD1 received in 1939 to cope with the dramatic increase in patronage, particularly to the military camps. Built in 1930 with Leyland 51-seat lowbridge body it was one of six similar vehicles purchased from that operator. It was rebodied by Strachans in 1949 and withdrawn in 1957. (L P Tancock collection)

Originally new to Maidstone & District in 1940, Silver Star No 17 (GKL 763) is a Leyland Titan TD7 with Weymann 54-seat bodywork. It was bought by Silver Star in May 1956 and before entering service was fitted with platform doors by Heaver for additional comfort on London express and Bournemouth excursion work.It was photographed in Blue Boar Row, Salisbury when working the Winterbourne and Allington route. (D A Elliott collection)

An all-Leyland vehicle was to be the first new double-decker for Silver Star. No 22 (EAM 776) was a Titan PD1 with 53-seat lowbridge body and was received by Silver Star in January 1947. It remained in stock until February 1962 when it was replaced by the fourth Leyland Atlantean delivered to the company. It is seen here at Winterbourne Earls en-route to Salisbury. (Dave Withers - L P Tancock collection)

In January 1951 Silver Star received Leyland PD2/1 No 18 (GWV 360) with 56-seat highbridge body which was later modified with platform doors by Heaver in 1954. Although sold to Wilts & Dorset, it went to Super Coaches of Upminster on the day Wilts & Dorset took over, and moved again when it was sold to A A Motors of Ayr. It is pictured at Blue Boar Row, Salisbury amid the fashions of the 1950s. (D A Elliott collection)

Negotiating one of the numerous low railway bridges around Salisbury is No 35 (TMW 853) at St Thomas's Bridge on the A30 road to London. Delivered in June 1959 this was the 13th Leyland Atlantean to be built and was completed with a Weymann 73-seat lowbridge body. The Atlantean revolutionised double-deck bus design by introducing rear-engined vehicles with driver-controlled front entrances. The vehicle did not remain with Wilts & Dorset but passed to Bristol Omnibus Company at Bristol for experimental trials which aided Bristol Commercial Vehicles in the planning of their rear-engined double-decker, the Bristol VRT, introduced some years later. (D A Elliott collection)

Proudly displaying its ownership is Leyland PSUC1/2 No 20 (LMW 483) which was new in January 1955. It carried a Burlingham Seagull body, finished with a central passenger doorway and 41 coach seats. Taken over on 5 June 1963 by Wilts & Dorset with the business, it was quickly sold on to Western National to become their No 3803. (D A Elliott collection)

40

Delivered to Silver Star in February 1958, No 33 was registered RAM 620 and was a Leyland Tiger Cub PSUC1/2 fitted with a Harrington 41-seat dual-purpose body. Seen here at Blue Boar Row, Salisbury with the old 'central' railway station in the background and the Silver Star emblem on the bus stop pole, the vehicle lasted with Wilts & Dorset after the takeover until February 1972. (D A Elliott collection)

The versatility of dual-purpose vehicles was important to Silver Star for the variety of work encompassed by the business. No 34 (SAM 47) was no exception, being a Leyland PSUC1/2 with Harrington 41-seat body, new in September 1958. Transferred to Wilts & Dorset ownership on 5 June 1963 it was rebuilt to 39-seat dual-purpose seating capacity in December 1969 and withdrawn from service on 30 September 1971. Note the smart new livery. (D A Elliott collection)

Clearly showing the smart application of Silver Star's red and silver livery is Leyland Atlantean PDR1/1 No 40 (XMW 706). It was received after the company had been refused permission by the Traffic Commissioners to use such vehicles on express routes. The high expense of fitting the vehicle as a 61-seat coach was not recouped as it was unable to earn its keep with the planned high-mileage revenue runs associated with express services. New in June 1961 it was not used by Wilts & Dorset but passed to Super Coaches of Upminster. (D A Elliott collection)

The unusual window shape and the dorsal fin on the rear of the Harrington body fitted to No 907 (SAM 47), which was originally Silver Star No 34, can be clearly seen in this view taken at Bournemouth Bus Station on 6 June 1970. (Mike Walker)

Chapter Five: Venture Forth to Nationalization and NBC

A major operator acquired by Wilts & Dorset after the Second World War was Venture Ltd based in Basingstoke which was taken over on 1 January 1951. This company had been operating buses in and around Basingstoke since May 1926 during the General Strike. Trade during this period was encouraging for the owner, Tom Thornycroft, who was also involved in the family business of manufacturing vehicle chassis.

Needless to say, advantage was made to test certain chassis from their own production lines in addition to those from other manufacturers for comparison. Business continued to improve to the extent that the single-deck fleet was no longer suitable by 1937. A number of AEC double-deckers were the eventual choice and the AEC marque remained the standard supplier right up until 1950.

The decision over which manufacturer to select to supply the double-deck replacements is intriguing and well worth detailing here. Early in 1937 letters were sent to AEC, Leyland, Thornycroft and Dennis chassis manufacturers requesting quotations for the supply of six double-deck buses. Dennis was so keen to get the contract that they had a demonstrator vehicle outside the Venture offices the next afternoon followed by one from AEC on the Wednesday evening complete with driver. It was a remarkable achievement as the letters from Venture had only been sent on the Monday.

After due consideration the choice was reduced to either AEC or Leyland. Because the ultimate decision was so difficult, a special luncheon was held to which these tenderers were invited. During the lunch a draw took place which the AEC representatives won, resulting in Regent chassis being ordered which were bodied by Park Royal. It is difficult to imagine a more novel way of placing an order for the supply of vehicles.

In March 1945 Venture Ltd was acquired by Red & White United Transport Ltd of Chepstow in South Wales and other than a number of new AEC double-deckers being bodied by Lydney Coachworks, another Red & White company, there was outwardly very little evidence of any change. The takeover of Red & White's bus interests into the British Transport Commission in February 1950 resulted in the control of Venture Ltd being transferred to Wilts & Dorset.

From the 1950s the rapid increase in car and television ownership greatly affected the use of buses, and public transport in general, particularly in connection with travel to work and evening entertainment. Audiences at cinemas were falling especially after the introduction of commercial television in various areas of Great Britain over the period from 1955 to the early 1960s. The new style of broadcasting supported with revenue gained from advertisers found support despite the serious doubts expressed by a number of Members of Parliament and other prominent people.

The 'adverts' themselves became a particular attraction for many and the style of presentation itself was welcomed as an alternative to that provided by the BBC. Independent Television was definitely here to stay and affected bus patronage dramatically as more and more people chose to stay at home and watch television instead of travelling to the cinema.

As the austerity of the Second World War waned and the wealth of individuals improved, the freedom offered by car ownership was sampled and found to be irresistible by many families. This situation has continued to gain pace until the present time with the resulting traffic congestion and road-building programme to satisfy these aspirations. Bus patronage continued to decrease, leading to reductions in service levels and the withdrawal of complete routes in many cases, particularly in the less populated rural areas.

As mentioned earlier, Wilts & Dorset Motor Services Ltd was a private company with a limited number of shareholders. In June 1920 it was converted to a public company in which many local people took up the option of purchasing shares. This, in effect, meant that the business was completely controlled locally with no influence over policy and practices from outside the area. The Southern Railway had been concerned at the effects of bus services on parallel railway lines and, therefore, wished to have some representation at Board level on as many bus companies as possible. Their desire was met in April 1931 when agreements were reached and signed by Wilts & Dorset, Southern Railway and Tilling & British Automobile Traction Ltd. The new partners obtained substantial shareholdings together with Board representation which the Southern Railway had been desperately seeking for some time.

The shareholding situation remained stable until the division of the Tilling and BAT interests in September 1942 when Wilts & Dorset became a Tilling-owned Company. These interests were transferred to the British Transport Commission in 1948 as a consequence of the 1947 Transport Act. This occurred in September 1948 when all Tilling's transport interests were sold to the BTC for £24,800,000 thus creating the first taste of nationalization for the bus-operating industry. Matters appeared to remain fairly stable until the Transport Act of 1962 disbanded the BTC and formed the Transport Holding Company which was set up to take over all the responsibilities previously vested in the BTC.

These latest arrangements were short-lived, however, as in 1967 the way was being prepared for the formation of the National Bus Company on 1 January 1969 as the result of the then Labour government's 1968 Transport Act .

One of the consequences of the formation of NBC was that the Wilts & Dorset fleetname was withdrawn from the fleet and letterheads from the early 1970s in order to comply with the corporate image directives from NBC headquarters. The only saving grace as far as purists were concerned was that at least the buses would be painted "a sort of red" even though they would be displaying Hants & Dorset fleetnames.

Control of Wilts & Dorset had passed to Hants & Dorset Motor Services in April 1964 but had been run as a separate subsidiary with a separate identity. Although carrying Hants & Dorset fleetnames, vehicles originally owned and licensed by Wilts & Dorset were not transferred and licensed to Hants & Dorset until 1972.

Originally a London Transport vehicle, No 12 (UU 6650) was an AEC Regal fitted with a London General Omnibus Company 29-seat open-platform body when new in 1929. The body was replaced with a Reading and Company Ltd open-platform body in January 1946. Pictured at the Venture garage in Basingstoke it was purchased by that company in January 1940 and passed to Wilts & Dorset in May 1951, being withdrawn from service in October 1953. (David J N Pennels - D A Elliott collection)

Purchased from City of Oxford Motor Services in April 1940, Venture No 41 (JO 5401) was built in 1932. An AEC Regent with a Park Royal 52-seat highbridge body, it was rebodied in late 1948 with a 1945 East Lancs body transferred from Venture No 60, another AEC Regent. Renumbered 441 by Wilts & Dorset it continued on the fleet strength until October 1954 having been further rebuilt in November 1951. (D A Elliott collection)

New to Venture in March 1937 was No 30 (BOU 700), an AEC Regent originally fitted with a Park Royal 56-seat highbridge body which was rebuilt by Red & White, another company in the group which owned Venture, in March 1948. Passing to Wilts & Dorset with the Venture business in January 1951 it became No 430 and lasted until August 1953. Note the unusual road sign. (D A Elliott collection)

Another vehicle purchased new by Venture was No 34 (COT 547), an AEC Regal with open-platform Park Royal 31-seat bodywork, which was modified by Red & White in December 1947 and again by Wilts & Dorset after takeover. It survived in this form until it was withdrawn in February 1956. (D A Elliott collection)

Above left: Heavily rebuilt in July 1951 by Wilts & Dorset as a 32-seat rear-entrance single-deck bus, No 36 (COT 549) was originally built in May 1938 as an AEC Regal 32-seat coach with Park Royal bodywork. As Wilts & Dorset's No 436 it continued in service until August 1956. (Bill Cannings collection)

Looking decidedly uneasy with the height available under the railway bridge crossing Chapel Hill (to the left) and Basingstoke Railway Station approach (on the right) is AEC Regent No 445 (ECG 646). Originally numbered 45 in the Venture fleet and new in September 1942 it carried a Willowbrook 56-seat rear-entrance body. It transferred with the Venture business on 1 January 1951. The chassis was classified as 'unfrozen' and equipped with an AEC 7.7 litre diesel engine with the body to Ministry of Supply specification, without a window in the upper deck rear emergency exit, although this was added in 1944 by Venture. The original slatted wooden seats, fitted only to the upper deck, were replaced by upholstered seats. The vehicle was removed from service in November 1954. (R F Mack - L P Tancock collection)

Below left: Austere bodywork by Willowbrook seating 56 passengers to Ministry of Supply specifications was fitted to AEC Regent No 45 (ECG 646) supplied to Venture in September 1942. It became Wilts & Dorset No 445 and was withdrawn in August 1954. (D A Elliott collection)

Received by Venture in April 1947, No 83 (FOT 204) was an AEC Regal with Duple 35-seat bodywork which was later rebuilt by Wilts & Dorset in January 1955. It remained in the fleet until September 1961 and found further work afterwards in South Wales. (D A Elliott collection)

Swanage Railway Station is the setting for No 484 (FOU 719) which was originally Venture No 84. It is an AEC Regal II, new in July 1947 with Duple 35-seat coach body. It was removed from the fleet in September 1958 and is seen on 4 August 1957. (P J Relf - D A Elliott collection)

Differences in the height of highbridge and lowbridge vehicles demonstrated by No 481 (FOT 202), an AEC Regent III, from April 1947. Equipped with a body built by Lydney Coachworks, a Red & White subsidiary, to a Weymann 56-seat highbridge design, it stands alongside Bristol KSW5G No 378 (JMW 955) which was with Wilts & Dorset from August 1953 until May 1972. Seen at Basingstoke, No 481 lasted in service until September 1962. (D A Elliott collection)

Displaying the Venture fleetname well is No 80 (FOT 201). Sister to the bus above and fitted with an AEC six cylinder 9.6 litre engine, it was completed with a preselect gearbox. Becoming No 480 in the Wilts & Dorset fleet on 1 January 1951, it was new in April 1947 and lasted until August 1962, being sold to a Gloucester dealer in October that year. (L P Tancock collection)

AEC Regent III No 93 (GCG 814) was another vehicle built by Lydney Coachworks to Weymann design, again with 56 seats in a highbridge layout. Becoming No 493 when joining Wilts & Dorset in 1951 it remained working until September 1962 and was pictured at Basingstoke on the Andover service. (D A Elliott collection)

After Venture was purchased by Wilts & Dorset a number of vehicles did not pass to the company, including No 106 (HOT 394), a Guy Arab III with Duple 57-seat bodywork. New in June 1950 it passed to Newbury & District, part of the Thames Valley company, in December 1950, before the takeover by Wilts & Dorset. These buses were thought by many to be extremely pleasing to look at with a stylish finish to the vehicle's exterior. (D A Eliott collection)

NOTICE TO PASSENGERS

Whilst our Staff are, as always, instructed to make every effort to avoid early running, the present difficulty in obtaining reliable watches makes it no longer possible to maintain the same high standard of accurate time-keeping as in pre-war days.

To avoid disappointment, passengers should be at their boarding point at least FIVE MINUTES before the advertised time of departure of the bus by which they desire to travel.

BUS STOPS

WITHIN BUILT-UP AREAS

(i.e., where traffic is restricted to 30 m.p.h.)
Buses will stop to pick up and set down at Passengers' request at Authorized Bus Stop Signs only.

OUTSIDE BUILT-UP AREAS

(i.e., in Country Districts where traffic is not restricted to 30 m.p.h.)
Buses will stop to pick up and set down Passengers at any point, subject to conditions of Road Safety, Steep Hill, etc. Passengers are requested to assist by congregating at Bus Stop Posts where possible.

WILTS & DORSET
MOTOR SERVICES LIMITED

FORMATION OF QUEUES

Passengers are advised that where six or more persons are waiting to board a bus they must form a queue, not more than two abreast, facing the direction of approach of the vehicle and must enter the vehicle in the order they stand in the queue

(Regulation of Traffic, Formation of Queues, No. 2 Order, 1942)

FARE DISPUTES

Passengers are reminded that Conductors are instructed to charge the fares printed in the Company's Official Fare Charts and Notices, also to enforce the Conditions relating to such fares as published in the Regulations and Conditions under "Concession Tickets."

In cases of dispute between passengers and the Conductor regarding the correct fare to be charged, or the acceptance of return tickets or other Concession tickets, passengers are requested to pay the fare asked for by the Conductor and to refer any matter of dispute to the Traffic Manager's Office, 8 Endless Street, Salisbury, where a refund will be made if it is found that the Conductor is in error.

Passengers may ask to see the official current Fare Chart and/or additional Fare Supplement as published in the Staff copy of the Time Table, both of which when applicable must be carried by Conductors at all times when on duty.

With triple bars across the rear lower-deck stair window behind the conductor in winter style uniform, No 191 (CHR 490) growls into Salisbury Bus Station with a healthy load. A Bristol K5G with Eastern Coach Works 52-seat lowbridge body, it survived from January 1940 until December 1958. (Bristol Vintage Bus Group)

Taken on 11 September 1948, this photograph shows Bristol K5G No 198 (CHR 497) with Eastern Coach Works 52-seat lowbridge body which had been new in January 1940. It continued in service until August 1959 although the body was rebuilt by Wilts & Dorset in February 1953. Two employees of the Engineering Department are pictured with the vehicle. (Bill Cannings collection)

Photographed during a layover period at Marlborough is No 194 (CHR 493). A Bristol K5G with Eastern Coach Works lowbridge 52-seat body, it was new in January 1940, rebuilt by Wilts & Dorset in October 1953 and sold to Esso for use at its Fawley refinery in October 1959, one month after withdrawal. (R F Mack - L P Tancock collection)

The first post-war delivery of vehicles involved two Bristol K5Gs with Eastern Coach Works 55-seat low-bridge bodies. The first was DMR 836, carrying fleet number 264, pictured in Salisbury Bus Station after destination display modification in April 1955. It was new in March 1946 and remained in service until November 1962. Note that the upper cream band has been terminated at the sides unlike the sister bus behind. (D A Elliott collection)

Parked in the sunshine outside the old garage in Castle Street Salisbury is No 267 (DMR 839), a Bristol K5G new in May 1946 with Eastern Coach Works 55-seat lowbridge body with open platform. Orinally equipped with destination indicators not only at the front and at the rear but also over the platform, the side display was removed in 1953 and the standard three-aperture display was replaced by the 'T' style equipment seen here when the body was rebuilt by Wilts & Dorset in February 1956. The bus was sold in December 1962. Note the other Bristol double decks inside the garage. (R F Mack - L P Tancock collection)

The later style of destination display including a three-track numeral box was fitted to Bristol K6B No 269 (EAM 612) in June 1956. New in April 1947 it continued in the fleet until November 1962 and is seen here in Bournemouth Bus Station on 3 August 1958 with a variety of Hants & Dorset Bristol Ks. (P J Relf - D A Elliott collection)

Entering service in December 1948, No 288 (FAM 5) was a Bristol K6B carrying an Eastern Coach Works 55-seat lowbridge body and originally allocated to Blandford depot for the lengthy Salisbury to Weymouth service. Seen here in later years at Andover Bus Station with the 'T' style destination display fitted in February 1957, it was withdrawn in the mid-1960s. (D A Elliott collection)

In its rebuilt form, having had its full drop windows replaced by sliding vents and its destination box redesigned, No 278 (EMW 283), a Bristol L6B with Beadle 32-seat coach body, is seen on private hire work. New in April 1949, the vehicle was sold to Sutherland Hydraulic and Machinery Company after withdrawal in November 1962. (Bristol Vintage Bus Group)

Below left: Lasting until the mid-1960s, No 283 (EMW 288) was a Bristol K5G with Eastern Coach Works 55-seat lowbridge bodywork which was delivered in March 1948. Seen here in original condition in Fore Street, Trowbridge on Service 24, the side destination box can be distinguished over the rear platform. These were removed from the batch of vehicles so fitted in 1953 and 1954. (Bristol Vintage Bus Group)

Displaying two versions of the Wilts & Dorset coach livery are Nos 296 and 297 (GAM 215 and 216). The original version included a maroon flash which was later changed to cream before rebuilding with sliding window vents and revised destination box in 1958. These Bristol L6B coaches with Portsmouth Aviation 32-seat bodywork were received in January 1950 and lasted until October 1961 (No 296) and January 1962 (No 297). (Bristol Vintage Bus Group/D A Elliott collection)

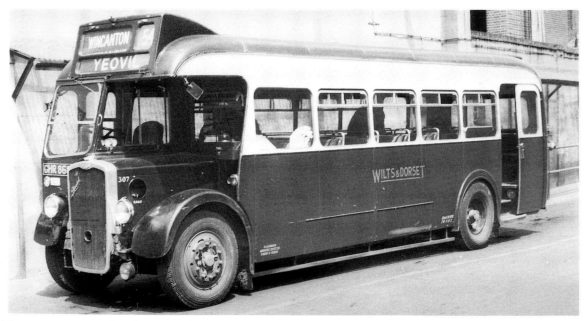

Awaiting passengers for the Yeovil route via Wincanton at Salisbury Bus Station is Bristol L6B No 307 (GHR 868). Equipped with rear-entrance Eastern Coach Works 35-seat body it was delivered in June 1950 and remained in service until withdrawal in November 1958. Other similar vehicles were returned to service to cover vehicle deficiencies during a rebodying programme but No 307 had already been sold to the Junior Leaders Regiment of the Royal Signals at Newton Abbott. (Bristol Vintage Bus Group)

Fashions of the 1950s, alongside a 'period piece' fire engine and bus, fill this scene. Note also the bus stop plate above the boy's head. No 199 (CHR 498), a Bristol K5G with Eastern Coach Works lowbridge 52-seat bodywork, operating a Milton Road journey, is seen in Exeter Street, Salisbury having sustained a small fire in the wooden slatted floor, caused by a lighted cigarette, which was extinguished by the fire brigade. The bus was new in January 1940 and withdrawn in October 1959, the body having been modified by Wilts & Dorset in April 1953. (Bill Cannings collection)

Standard deliveries to Tilling companies after the Second World War consisted mainly of Bristol and Eastern Coach Works variants. One such delivery in July 1950 was No 312 (GMR 27) a Bristol K5G with 55-seat lowbridge body. By the time that this photograph was taken in Basingstoke a modified destination display had been fitted in August 1960. The upper deck style of seating four passengers abreast on each bench was unpopular with both conductors and passengers. (D A Elliott collection)

No 314 (GMR 893) was a Bristol KS6B fitted with Eastern Coach Works 55-seat lowbridge body and received by the company in October 1950. The 'T' style destination equipment was installed in March 1961 and the bus is seen at Basingstoke where it spent its working life. (D A Elliott collection)

Cigarettes were freely advertised in the 1960s when No 357 (HMR 809) a Bristol KSW5G with Eastern Coach Works 55-seat body was caught at Basingstoke Railway Station. Three shillings and ten old pence for twenty cigarettes is approximately equivalent to 19p. Delivered in April 1952, it lasted until withdrawn in 1972. (D A Elliott collection)

Pictured at leafy Bournemouth Bus Station on 8 August 1954 is Bristol KSW5G No 339 (HHR 751) which had been received in December 1951. Carrying the usual Eastern Coach Works 55-seat lowbridge body, these passengers would be accommodated with 27 on the upper deck and 28 on the lower. The KSW model differed from the K and KS versions in being 8 feet wide rather than 7 feet 6 inches. (P J Relf - D A Elliott collection)

Many of the KSWs eventually ended up allocated to Basingstoke, replacing worn-out stock inherited from the purchase of Venture. An example from the 1952 delivery is No 367 (JAM 420), a KSW6B with the typical Eastern Coach Works 55-seat lowbridge body, which was withdrawn in May 1971. (Bristol Vintage Bus Group)

Thirty-foot length vehicles were the exception rather than the rule in the early 1950s. A number of Bristol LL6Bs were delivered, including No 323 (GMW 913), in January 1951 complete with Eastern Coach Works 39-seat rear-entrance bodies. For some years it was used in the Romsey area and is seen here at Stockbridge on Service 83 but in latter years was used on contract work in the Basingstoke and Andover areas. (D A Elliott collection)

The rear destination display on Leyland Lion LT2 carrying registration number MW 7053 in the background of this photograph is of particular interest. The 32-seat body was fitted by Wilts & Dorset to this vehicle in 1946. In the foreground is the main subject No 504 (BOW 169) which was a Bristol L5G

new to Hants & Dorset in 1938 and purchased by Wilts & Dorset in February 1952. Carrying a Beadle body, modified to seat 32 passengers by Hants & Dorset in 1950, it continued in service until September 1955. (Bristol Vintage Bus Group)

Crosville exchanged ten single-deck Leyland Tiger TS7 buses for ten surplus Leyland TD1 double-deck buses with Wilts & Dorset in April 1952. One vehicle received in this exchange was No 511 (BFM 204) which carried Eastern Coach Works 32-seat front-entrance bodywork and remained in service with Wilts & Dorset until October 1954. (Bristol Vintage Bus Group)

Dual-doorway buses are not a modern idea as evidenced by No 536 (JMR 85) at Bournemouth Bus Station on 30 July 1953. The rear doorway was removed in March 1955 and the capacity increased from 39 coach seats to 41. Received in April 1953, it lasted with the company until October 1972 having been renumbered to 759 in September 1971. A Bristol LS6G, it carried Eastern Coach Works bodywork. (Vectis Transport Publications - D A Elliott collection)

Seen after modification in May 1954 from dual-door to single-door layout is Bristol LS6G No 530 (JHR 389) at Victoria Coach Station in London complete with coach-style seating for express work. The driver is changing the destination blind display for the return journey in the days before corporate image and National Express. Delivered in February 1953, it lasted with Wilts & Dorset until October 1972 by which time it was used as a one-man-operated bus and renumbered 753. (D A Elliott collection)

Below and right: Wilts & Dorset was very capable of carrying out some extensive body work at Salisbury Garage and during World War Two these premises were utilised for assisting with aircraft production in the war effort. An example of the capabilities of the workforce is shown here where Bristol LWL5Gs were rebuilt for one-man-operation, oddly enough, after receipt of specifically designed underfloor-engined vehicles ideal for this style of operation. All three vehicles in these photographs were delivered in October 1954 and all modified in 1959 to the full front design. No 558 (LAM 108) is seen at Salisbury Bus Station in original condition; No 559 (LAM 109) at Basingstoke Bus Station in the renovated style and No 566 (LHR 857) undergoing modification at Salisbury Garage. Colloquially known by staff as 'conker boxes' after this work, they remained in service with the Company in some cases up until the early 1970s. (No 566 P Trevaskis - all D A Elliott collection)

Severe front end damage was sustained by No 533 (JHR 604) a Bristol LS6G with Eastern Coach Works 39-seat dual-purpose front-entrance bodywork, new in January 1953. After repair the vehicle returned to work until being withdrawn in March 1972, having been renumbered 756. (Bill Cannings collection)

Summer uniform is being worn by the conductor of No 385 (JWV 849), a Bristol KSW6B, on 31 July 1971 in New Canal at Salisbury. The bus, carrying Eastern Coach Works 55-seat lowbridge bodywork with platform doors and staggered upper-deck seating, was new in October 1953 and withdrawn in 1972. The open windscreen and windows indicate the heat on the day. (P J Relf - D A Elliott collection)

Right: White covers were issued to drivers and conductors for use on their uniform caps during the summer seasons in Tilling days. White summer jackets were also issued as seen on one member of the conducting staff in this view at Salisbury Bus Station. Nos 333 (HHR 60) and 337 (HHR 64) were both Bristol KSW5Gs with Eastern Coach Works 55-seat lowbridge bodies new in November 1952. (D A Elliott collection)

Below: Bristol KSW6B No 382 (JWV 381) was delivered in 1953 but a month earlier than No 386 (see right) although it incorporated similar improvements. It sustained accident damage in November 1962 and the front destination indicator was modified to the 'T' style during repairs. Seen passing the George Hotel in Amesbury on 19 April 1963 it survived a further nine years, being withdrawn in 1972. (P J Relf - D A Elliott collection)

Above: The lengthy route between Salisbury and Swindon was numbered 709 due to it being jointly operated by Bristol Omnibus Company (Service 70 Swindon - Marlborough) and Wilts & Dorset (Service 9 Salisbury - Marlborough). From 1953 in common with other long-distance services based on Salisbury the route was given the first double-deckers equipped with platform doors. Upstairs seating was also improved on these buses with staggered seats to ensure that passengers were sat four rather than three across each bench. No 386 (JWV 978), a KSW6B with Eastern Coach Works 55-seat lowbridge body, was new in October 1953 and withdrawn in 1972. It is seen in Swindon awaiting the return run back to Salisbury. (D A Elliott collection)

Early delivered Bristol Lodekkas incorporated long slats on the radiator grille exemplified by No 603 (KMW 345) at Salisbury Bus Station. The design supplied all the highbridge body benefits within a lowheight design with seats either side of a central upper-deck gangway, rather than the four-abreast seating with sunken offside gangway as had been standard on the upper deck of lowbridge double-deck buses until the revolutionary Lodekka. No 603, received in May 1954, displays the full destination equipment of that time. The first 17 Lodekkas supplied to Wilts & Dorset were allocated to Salisbury City services remaining with the Company until withdrawn by Hants & Dorset in June 1975. No 603's destination has been set for its next scheduled run on Service 59 to Devizes Road Extension. (D A Elliott collection)

Coronation Year 1953 was celebrated throughout the Empire and Wilts & Dorset was no exception as seen in this patriotic display on the front of Castle Street Garage in Salisbury with a Bristol L6B with Portsmouth Aviation bodywork parked on the forecourt, almost masking a new Bristol LS. (Bill Cannings collection)

In pristine condition at Salisbury Garage is No 607 (LMR 740), alongside No 608 (LMR 741), both Bristol LD6B models with Eastern Coach Works 58-seat open-platform lowheight bodies. Note the painted Corona advertisement applied before entry into revenue-earning service in January 1955. Both vehicles carry the long slatted grilles standard on Lodekkas at the time and the three-section destination display. The label in the cab windscreen reads DELICENSED. This bus continued to work for about 20 years. (Bristol Vintage Bus Group)

The standard vehicle for Salisbury City Services during the later 1950s was the Bristol LD. With modified front grille and destination box, No 606 (LHR 155), a Bristol-engined example, basks in the sunshine between trips at Salisbury Bus Station. It saw service with Wilts & Dorset between October 1954 and December 1973, being taken out of use by Hants & Dorset. Note the differing upper-deck opening windows and destination display styles on the two Lodekkas in this scene. (D A Elliott collection)

Formerly a Leyland Titan TD1 bus with Short Brothers 50-seat highbridge bodywork and numbered 243, UF 7407 was acquired from Southdown in June 1939 and converted into a breakdown truck in February 1940. It survived in its revised role until March 1961 and is seen on duty in Salisbury Bus Station. (Bristol Vintage Bus Group)

Opposite (top): Operating to West Harnham from Blue Boar Row in Salisbury on a particularly wet day is Bristol LD6B No 612 (LMW 915) which was new in March 1955 and survived until February 1975. The length of service to the company is praise indeed to the durability of the Bristol/Eastern Coach Works product. The Pools win seems small fry compared to the National Lottery's millions. (D A Elliott collection)

Opposite (bottom): Built as one-man-operated vehicles were a number of Bristol LS5Gs carrying Eastern Coach Works 41-seat bus-style bodies as exemplified by this view of No 585 (OAM 366) at Salisbury Bus Station loading up for Hindon on Service 26. Delivered in September 1956 it remained in use until October 1974. (D A Elliott collection)

Today, Wilts & Dorset uses Bristol LH single-deck buses for driver training which are used on stage carriage work when not required by the Driver Training Schools at Poole or Salisbury. In earlier days vehicles were specifically converted and allocated full-time for driver training including No 9094 (KMW 109) seen here at Grosvenor Square, Southampton in the mid-1970s. This Bristol LD6G was one of the first three Lodekkas bought by Wilts & Dorset in March 1954 as No 602. It was converted to a driver training bus in March 1974 and carried a special livery to attract candidates to join Hants & Dorset when the staffing position was causing problems. (D A Elliott collection)

LS6G No 525 (JAM 304) stands at Alton railway station. At the time of the photograph it had been downgraded from dual-purpose work to stage-carriage duties and was operating to Basingstoke on Service 107 via Bentworth and Lasham with a seating capacity of 41 passengers. It served Wilts & Dorset for almost 20 years between December 1952 and April 1972. It was renumbered 748 in September 1971 and had increased its capacity from 39 to 41 seats in April 1955 upon removal of the rear doorway. (Bristol Vintage Bus Group)

Wintry conditions make the going difficult for Bristol LD6G No 623 (OHR 124). Fitted with Eastern Coach Works 60-seat body complete with platform doors for country services, it is seen enroute from Marlborough to Salisbury and traverses the tricky road surface somewhere on Salisbury Plain. The steamed-up windows indicate that there is life on board the vehicle which was received in November 1956 and withdrawn in June 1970 following an accident sustained in June 1969. (D A Elliott collection)

Originally introduced with improved seating to compete with British Railways between Salisbury and Southampton in October 1957, No 631 (PMR 914) is a Bristol LD6G with Eastern Coach Works 60-seat low-height bodywork and conductor-operated manual platform doors. Seen in later life on Service 24 between Warminster and Salisbury it lasted in service until April 1976. (D A Elliott collection)

Beneath the trolleybus wires at Bournemouth Square on 11 June 1968 is No 637 (UAM 941) on Service 38 from Salisbury. It carries hopper ventilators on both the front and side windows on its Eastern Coach Works 60-seat body with platform doors. An LD6G model new in November 1959, it lasted well into the 1970s. Trolleybuses were withdrawn in Bournemouth during April 1969. (Mike Walker)

Built in 1962, No 649 (687 AAM) is a Bristol FS6B with Eastern Coach Works 60-seat lowheight body complete with platform doors. Seen in Marlborough High Street around 1970 the bus is already prepared for its return journey on Service 5. (P Trevaskis - Jeremy Weller collection)

Representing the style of coaching stock from the 1950s is Bristol MW6G No 703 (RMR 524) with Eastern Coach Works 39-seat coach bodywork, new in July 1958. It was renumbered 803 in September 1971 and used as a dual-purpose 37-seat vehicle in its latter days until withdrawn in February 1975. (D A Elliott collection)

By the time that this photograph was taken in Marlborough on 28 September 1968, No 705 (RMR 992) had been rebuilt from a 39-seater coach to a standard bus seating 32 passengers with room for an authorised 25 standing. In this guise the vehicle lasted into the 1970s. (Mike Walker)

In full cream Wilts & Dorset coach livery is No 714 (XMR 947), a Bristol MW6G with Eastern Coach Works 39-seat coach body on a private hire outing. New in July 1961 it was withdrawn in August 1976 after having been used latterly as a dual-purpose vehicle. (D A Elliott collection)

Displaying the new style of Eastern Coach Works coach body for Bristol MWs is No 716 (674 AAM), an MW6G with 39-seat body. Delivered in May 1962 it was used initially on long-distance private hire and excursion work. It was withdrawn after 14 years in June 1976. (D A Elliott collection)

Bedford coaches entered service with Wilts & Dorset as a result of Eastern Coach Works being heavily involved in processing large orders for Lodekkas. No 912 (BMW 137C) was a Bedford SB13 built in 1965 to carry 41 passengers in a Duple body. Seen about to depart with a tour from Salisbury Bus Station the vehicle lasted until January 1974. (D A Elliott collection)

Basingstoke Garage is the location for Bristol MW6G No 833 (EMR 298D) which was originally No 723 when it was delivered in 1966. Carrying an Eastern Coach Works 41-seat dual-purpose body it continued in service until February 1977. (D A Elliott collection)

Taken over with the Silver Star business in June 1963 was No 903 (RAM 620) a Leyland Tiger Cub PSUC1/2 built in 1958 and originally Silver Star No 33. It is seen at Salisbury Bus Station in Wilts & Dorset livery on 6 June 1970. It carried a Harrington 41-seat dual-purpose body and was withdrawn in 1971. (Mike Walker)

Seen outside the Dorset County Museum in Dorchester on Service 34 between Weymouth and Salisbury is Leyland Leopard L2 No 908 (WAM 441). Built in 1960 with this Harrington 39-seat dual-purpose body it was formerly Silver Star No 38. It was in service with Wilts & Dorset from 5 June 1963 to May 1972. (D A Elliott collection)

A pair of Leyland Tiger Cub PSUC1/2s stand in Salisbury Garage. Both were new to Silver Star and joined Wilts & Dorset on 5 June 1963 . No 902 (PMW 386) was originally No 32 with Silver Star and No 901 (PHR 829) was No 31. The vehicles were new in 1957 and withdrawn in April 1971 (No 901) and July 1972 (No 902). (D A Elliott collection)

A comparison of vehicle types used on Salisbury City Services on 1 July 1967 catches Bristol KSW5G No 372 (JHR 883) with Eastern Coach Works 55-seat lowbridge body and open platform, operating a relief journey to Wilton on Service 60. Bristol LD6B No 606 (LHR 155) with Eastern Coach Works 58-seat open-platform lowheight body operates the service journey to Ditchampton from New Canal. No 372 was withdrawn in May 1969 and No 606 in December 1973. (M R Hodges)

On 6 September 1967 No 636 (TMW 273) was photographed at Durrington on Service 5 from Marlborough in sunny weather. It is a Bristol LD6G carrying Eastern Coach Works 60-seat lowheight bodywork with platform doors. Delivered in September 1959 the bus lasted well into the 1970s. (M R Hodges)

Services were often scheduled to connect at Upavon (The Ship Inn) where No 667 (476 BMR) was photographed. A Bristol FS6B built in 1963, it carries Eastern Coach Works 60-seat lowheight bodywork associated with country services with platform doors. The crew await the arrival of the connecting bus. A very pleasant view, epitomising Wilts & Dorset in the late1960s. (M R Hodges)

Changing the front destination indicators in wet weather was a miserable task for conductors or drivers but no such problems on 6 September 1967 at Marlborough High Street. Equipped with staggered upper-deck seats in its Eastern Coach Works 55-seat lowbridge body with platform doors, No 387 (JWV 979) is a Bristol KSW6B that was delivered in October 1953 for longer distance services. (M R Hodges)

Photographed on 6 September 1967 at The Ship Inn at Upavon is Bristol LS6G No 523 (JAM 227) with Eastern Coach Works bodywork, by this time upgraded to carry 41 passengers. It was new in November 1952, converted for one-man-operation in August 1958 and withdrawn by 1971. (M R Hodges)

Fitted with camel-back semi-coach seating to compete with British Railways on the route between Salisbury and Southampton, No 632 (PWV 353) was delivered in January 1958. A Bristol LD6G with Eastern Coach Works 60-seat rear entrance body it carried platform doors for its regular long-distance runs. In September 1971 it was renumbered 432 and withdrawn in April 1976. Captured on its regular haunt at Southampton Bus Station, the shape of the seating can be seen, as can a conductor carrying his ticket machine box. (D A Elliott collection)

Hopper-style windows, rear platform doors and camel-back semi-coach seating feature on Bristol LD6G No 636 (TMW 273) pictured at Salisbury Bus Station. Received by Wilts & Dorset in September 1959, it carried Eastern Coach Works 60-seat bodywork and was renumbered 436 in September 1971. It was withdrawn from stock in November 1975. (D A Elliott collection)

White window rubbers were the vogue when Bristol FS6G No 638 (676 AAM) was delivered to Wilts & Dorset in September 1962. Carrying the usual Eastern Coach Works 60-seat body with platformdoors it was photographed at Bournemouth Bus Station. The offside illuminated advertisement panel, also a short-lived fashion of the early 1960s, can clearly be seen. (D A Elliott collection)

Cave Brown Cave radiator systems could easily be identified on buses by the radiators positioned either side of the destination box. On the right, No 666 (475 BMR), a Bristol FS6B built in 1963 with this system, can be compared with one not so fitted. No 640 (678AAM) is a Bristol FS6G which became Hants & Dorset No 103 in September 1971 and was removed from service in January 1980. The buses are seen parked up in Salisbury Garage. Of the four car marques advertised, only one is now available and that but a shadow of its former self (D A Elliott collection)

Warm weather has encouraged the driver of No 655 (693 AAM) to open up the windscreen in New Canal, Salisbury on 31 July 1971. Fitted with an open rear platform and intended for Salisbury City Services it is seen operating to Wilton (Ditchampton). This Bristol FS6B with Eastern Coach Works 60-seat body was received in May 1963, renumbered 118 in September 1971 and withdrawn in August 1976. (P J Relf - D A Elliott collection)

The very first Bristol FLF delivered to Wilts & Dorset was No 658 (467 BMR), a Gardner-engined variant with Eastern Coach Works 70-seat front-entrance bodywork. Seating was in the camel-back semi-coach style and the vehicle entered service in 1963. It was renumbered 201 in September 1971 and withdrawn in March 1980. It is seen at Salisbury Bus Station after arriving on Service 38 from Bournemouth. (D A Elliott collection)

The last batch of Bristol FS buses to be received were not fitted with the camel-back semi-coach seats that were fitted to the Bristol FLFs delivered earlier. FS No 664 (473 BMR), delivered in 1963, was a Bristol-engined variant and carried Eastern Coach Works 60-seat bodywork with platform doors. Equipped with an offside illuminated advertisement panel and Cave Brown Cave heating and ventilation system, the bus is seen at Andover Bus Station. Renumbered 121 in September 1971 it was removed from the Hants & Dorset fleet in June 1977. (D A Elliott collection)

Standard seating was fitted to later Bristol FLF vehicles for Wilts & Dorset including No 680 (EMR296D), bought in 1966. Waiting for its next scheduled run to Swindon on Service 470 (previously 709), it is seen in the parking area at Salisbury Bus Station. It was renumbered 215 by Hants & Dorset in September 1971 and withdrawn from the fleet in October 1980. (D A Elliott collection)

A number of Bristol FLFs were supplied with Leyland engines and semi-automatic gear boxes. One was No 687 (JMR 817F), built in 1967 with the usual Eastern Coach Works 70-seat body. Seen at Bournemouth Bus Station on 30 July 1971 before being renumbered 222 by Hants & Dorset in September of that year, it continued in service until July 1980. (Vectis Transport Publications - D A Elliott collection)

Unusual purchases in the 1960s included No 813 (HHR 943E) a Bedford VAM 14 with a Strachan 41-seat dual-doorway body. Built in 1967 it was renumbered 501 in September 1971 by Hants & Dorset and withdrawn in February 1974. It is seen in Andover Bus Station after arrival on Service 82.. (D A Elliott collection)

Further Bedfords were received in 1968 as exemplified by No 818 (LMR 738F), a VAM 70 with Willowbrook 40-seat dual-doorway body. Loading for Shaftesbury via Bowerchalke on Service 29 at Salisbury Bus Station, the bus was later renumbered to 506 by Hants & Dorset in September 1971 and taken out of service in October 1974. (D A Elliott collection)

Flat windscreens were standard on the earlier versions of the Bristol RE models. No 821 (MMW 351G) was an RELL6G built in 1969 and fitted with Eastern Coach Works 45-seat dual-doorway bodywork. It became No 601 in September 1971 under the Hants & Dorset renumbering scheme and is seen at Salisbury Bus Station. (M Bennett - D A Elliott collection)

Slightly deeper flat wind-screens were fitted to a number of Bristol RELL6Gs delivered to Wilts & Dorset including No 828 (PRU 63G) completed with Eastern Coach Works 45-seat dual-doorway bodywork. Delivered in June 1969 it is seen here in Christchurch High Street bound for Bournemouth after having been renumbered as 608 by Hants & Dorset. (D A Elliott collection)

Curved windscreens became standard on later Bristol RELLs including No 843 (TRU 944J), a Gardner-engined vehicle with the usual 45-seat dual-doorway body specified by Wilts & Dorset. It is seen at Andover Bus Station preparing to return to Salisbury on Service 80, possibly having come through from Newbury on that route. It was renumbered 617 by Hants & Dorset in September 1971. (D A Elliott collection)

Lightweight saloons included Bristol LH and Ford R1014 models both carrying similar Eastern Coach Works bodies although some Fords did carry Plaxton bodywork. An example of the Bristol LH6L specimens is No 837 (REL 748H), built in 1969, unusually with a 39-seat dual-doorway body rather than the normal 43-seat single-door variety delivered to most companies at the time. This bus became No 523 with Hants & Dorset in September 1971 and is seen on Service 17 at Marlborough. It was withdrawn in July 1977. (M Bennett - D A Elliott collection)

Twin-steer Bedford VAL 70 coaches were taken into Wilts & Dorset stock, including No 930 (SLJ 758H), new in June 1970 and fitted with a Duple 49-seat body. It became No 61 in September 1971 and was withdrawn in August 1976. (D A Elliott collection)

Two-axle coaches taken into the Wilts & Dorset fleet in June 1971 included No 21 (VLJ 413J), a Bedford YRQ with Duple 41-seat bodywork. Seen at Castle Street Garage in Salisbury it remained in service until July 1978. (D A Elliott collection)

Further twin-steer Bedford VAL 70 vehicles carrying Duple 49-seat bodywork came into the fleet during July 1971. Among them was No 63 (WEL 803J) which was later upgraded to 53 seats in January 1974 and withdrawn in November 1979. (D A Elliott collection)

Fourteen Leyland Panther PSUR1/1 buses with Willow-brook 49-seat bodies were bought from Maidstone & District during 1971 and 1972. Dating from 1967 they carried fleet numbers 684 to 699. No 699 (JKK 199E) shows its offside to the camera as it leaves Basingstoke Bus Station for East Oakley on 5 August 1972. (M R Hodges)

A nearside view of one of the Panthers is shown on No 693 (JKK 204E) at Basingstoke Bus Station. This particular vehicle remained in the fleet until May 1977.(D A Elliott collection)

Chapter Six: A Return to Wilts & Dorset

In preparation for the sale (privatisation) of the National Bus Company a number of the larger companies were broken up and new subsidiary companies were named. Hants & Dorset was divided into six parts. One of the principal bus operators created was to be called Hampshire Bus covering Basingstoke, Winchester, Southampton and Andover garages whilst another was to be called Wilts & Dorset Bus Company Ltd with garages at Poole, Salisbury, Ringwood, Blandford, Lymington, Pewsey and Swanage together with several outstations. The revival of the Wilts & Dorset fleetname was welcomed by many local individuals who felt that the return of the name reflected better the area that the new Company covered than did its predecessor. It was on 27 March 1983 that the new Wilts & Dorset was born. The Company was very keen to display its new name without delay and immediately set about removing the previous Hants & Dorset identities on their vehicles, properties and letterheads.

In effect the replacement of fleetnames on the buses merely required the HAN in Hants & Dorset being covered with vinyls carrying WIL to form the correct identity name. Occasionally, though, buses could be seen carrying just the wording TS & DORSET until the whole fleet could be completed.

There were a number of exceptionally happy winners and even more extremely disappointed losers in the bidding by interested parties in the sell-off of the National Bus Company subsidiaries by the government as a consequence of the 1985 Transport Act. The sale process was conducted by confidential sealed bids from a number of parties including potential competitors and management teams. Each bidder would have to take account of the problems to be faced in a newly deregulated bus industry, another equally important aspect of the 1985 Transport Act.

The neighbouring Hampshire Bus Company was purchased by Stagecoach of Perth who were later to become a major operator of buses and coaches in numerous areas of both England and Scotland, in addition to certain countries in Africa. The sale was concluded on 7 April 1987, some two months ahead of the sale of Wilts & Dorset.

A great deal of interest was shown in the offer of Wilts & Dorset for sale and included two rival management bids from Wilts & Dorset teams. One involved Hugh Malone, the Finance Director together with Andrew Bryce, Traffic Manager and Rodney Luxton, the Fleet Engineer. The other involved Alan Rolls, the Managing Director, who wished to pursue a bid in conjunction with the major Isle of Wight bus operator, Southern Vectis. The management team from Wilts & Dorset felt that their bid would offer more security for both the Company's future and that of its employees which at the time numbered approximately 600 staff.

The preferred bidder was announced as the management team led by Hugh Malone who became Wilts & Dorset's Managing & Finance Director. The sale was finalised in June 1987 when the deal was signed by himself, Douglas Smith CBE who became non-executive Chairman, Andrew Bryce who became Operations Director, Rodney Luxton who became Engineering Director, and the then Minister for Public Transport, David Mitchell. On 24 June 1987 Wilts & Dorset became a private Company, owned by the three directors who have since demonstrated a determination to survive even the most aggressive competition from other operators.

To distinguish the identity of the new Wilts & Dorset, a stylish livery of red, white and black was introduced, together with a corporate logo which is used on vehicles, signs, notices and stationery. At the time of the buy-out the newest vehicles were five Leyland Olympians with ECW dual-purpose seating delivered in February and March 1984 in the double-deck section, all based at Salisbury, and ten Leyland Tiger coaches equipped and liveried for National Express services in four instances and equipped with dual-purpose seating in the other six cases. These were mostly allocated to Salisbury and the northern district for private hire and other coaching duties. The Tigers were delivered to the Company between January and March 1985.

Launching the new Wilts & Dorset livery in summer 1987 with a champagne shower is Hugh Malone, the Managing and Finance Director of the company. The event took place in Blue Boar Row, Salisbury with Bristol VRT No 3325 receiving the benefits. (Wilts & Dorset Bus Company Ltd)

All smiles as the management team who became the new owners of Wilts & Dorset celebrate the completion of the deal on 24 June 1987. Standing from left to right are non-executive Chairman Douglas Smith CBE; Operations Director Andrew Bryce; the then Minister for Public Transport, David Mitchell, who dropped in to congratulate the team. together with Rodney Luxton, the Engineering Director. Hugh Malone (seated on the right) as Managing and Finance Director prepares to sign the deal on behalf of the successful team with an unknown representative of the Department of Transport. (Wilts & Dorset Bus Company Ltd)

The first new vehicles for the reborn Wilts & Dorset company were five Leyland Olympians and ten Leyland Tiger coaches. The Olympians were delivered during February and March 1984 and No 3903 (A903 JPR) is seen in original livery at Salisbury Bus Station, leaving for Bournemouth on Service 238 on 21 April 1984. The NBC logo is clearly visible together with the Transign destination display. The Eastern Coach Works body gave dual-purpose seating for 70 passengers. With the arrival of dual-purpose Optare Spectras during 1995 these vehicles are due to be refurbished with bus seating. (Martin S Curtis)

A comparison of the differing front end styles are seen in this evening view taken at Salisbury Bus Station on 23 January 1988. Both are Bristol RELL6Gs with Eastern Coach Works 50-seat dual-purpose bodywork. No 622 (XLJ 727K) has arrived from Bristol and Bath on Service X4 and No 623 (XLJ 728K) has arrived on Service 37 from Southampton. These buses were delivered in 1971. (Andrew Bissett)

Pictured at Bradford-on-Avon on its way to Bath and Bristol on the Service X4 journey from Salisbury on 23 January 1988 is No 622 (XLJ 727K). It was normal practice to allocate dual-purpose seated Bristol RELLs or Leyland Nationals to this lengthy route for passenger comfort. (Andrew Bissett)

Carrying the bland NBC unrelieved red livery with Wilts & Dorset fleetnames is No 627 (CRU 137L), a

Bristol RELL6G with Eastern Coach Works 45-seat dual-purpose bodywork, new in 1972. On Service 107 to Canford Heath, it is seen in Westover Road, Bournemouth. (Bristol Vintage Bus Group)

Dual-purpose livery in NBC style was still carried by Bristol RELL6G No 1647 (XLJ 722K) when it was photographed on 25 August 1989 on Weymouth front. It was new to Hants & Dorset in 1972. (Martin S Curtis)

Gardner engines were fitted to most Bristol VRTs in the Wilts & Dorset fleet. A Series 2 example is seen at Blue Boar Row in Salisbury operating Service 55 to West Harnham before the route's change to service by Skipper minibuses. No 3308 (NRU 308M) carried Eastern Coach Works 74-seat bodywork. Note the grille on the offside rear engine compartment and the company name attached to the front grille. (Bristol Vintage Bus Group)

Delivered in 1977, No 3368 (RJT 159R) is a Series 3 Bristol VRTSL/6G with Eastern Coach Works 74-seat body. Waiting time at Shaftesbury on Service 139 to Bournemouth Square, it still carries the NBC red livery when the photograph was taken. (Bristol Vintage Bus Group)

Transign destination equipment was experimented with on a number of vehicles in NBC fleets. One still carrying this on 18 February 1984 at Branksome Roundabout in Poole, when operating Service 109 between Bournemouth and Corfe Mullen, was No 3450 (KRU 850W), a Series 3 Bristol VRTSL/6G with Eastern Coach Works 74-seat body. (Martin S Curtis)

The livery for the privatised Wilts & Dorset fleet is displayed on Series 2 Bristol VRTSL/6G No 3325 (JJT 437N) at Blue Boar Row, Salisbury and compares favourably with the NBC red livery with single white stripe carried on No 3341 (JJT 443N) in the background. (Bristol Vintage Bus Group)

By the time this photograph was taken No 3348 had been renumbered into the low-mileage fleet as 4348 (NJT 34P) and was parked up at Lymington Garage before its next scheduled run. It was new to Hants & Dorset in 1976. (Bristol Vintage Bus Group)

A high number of Bristol LH6L buses with Eastern Coach Works bodies were bought from Bristol Omnibus Company in 1982. Included in those received was No 3841 (YAE 513V), caught by the photographer at Bournemouth Square on 30 May 1983 when operating Service 150 to Swanage. (Mike Walker)

Included in the same batch of secondhand LHs as 3841 was No 3856 (AFB 592V) which is seen on 25 August 1989 negotiating Weymouth seafront when operating a summer only service from Swanage. (Martin S Curtis)

Outside the Minster Cafe in Wimborne Square is Leyland National No 3722 (VFX 988S) operating Service 133 to Poole. It wears unrelieved NBC red with National Bus Company style fleet-name, albeit without the double N logo. It was new in February 1978 but has now been removed from the fleet. (Bristol Vintage Bus Group)

Ten miles from Salisbury at the delightfully named Teffont Evias is No 3307 (NRU 307M) a 1974 Bristol VRTSL/6G with Eastern Coach Works 74-seat body. Captured on its way to Hindon on a pleasant 10 September 1987 it was still in NBC poppy red livery. This bus was one of two painted in all over silver in 1977 to mark Queen Elizabeth II's Silver Jubilee and has now been withdrawn. (P Trevaskis)

A number of Leyland and Daimler Fleetlines were purchased by Wilts & Dorset from London Transport in the 1980s. One Leyland Fleetline acquired in 1983 was No 1932 (KJD 14P) carrying Metro Cammell Weymann 76-seat highbridge bodywork which had been new to London Transport in July 1976. Pictured near Cemetery Junction in Bournemouth while operating Service 133 to Wimborne and Poole, it has now been withdrawn from the fleet. (Bristol Vintage Bus Group)

One of the Daimler examples of the Fleetline is No 1940 (KUC 172P) carrying Park Royal 77-seat highbridge bodywork and acquired from London Transport in 1986. New in 1975, it is equipped with electronic destination display and is seen entering Poole Bus Station. (Bristol Vintage Bus Group)

Chapter Seven: Deregulation and Further Competition

An element of competition has always been an aspect of bus service provision. This had been accepted as part of the business and had been controlled by the Traffic Commissioners since the early 1930s. The 1985 Transport Act, implemented on 26 October 1986, was to pave the way for unprecedented assaults by competitors who,perhaps, saw the division in buy-out policies within the Company's management as an indication of weakness and a prime opportunity to take advantage by 'muscling in' on the Company's area.

How wrong these assumptions were is now part of bus industry history but is seen as a classic aggressive response to an attack on the Company. The initial attacks came from Badgerline with a gradually introduced competitive network of routes on Salisbury City services, resulting at one time in 24 buses operating each hour to Bemerton Heath housing estate on the western edge of the city. Throughout the competition period Wilts & Dorset retaliated with a sense of urgency and enthusiasm, the future of the Company depending on a stable and optimistic outlook.

Badgerline's routes were operated with a combination of 16-seat Ford Transit and new Iveco (Fiat) minibuses, completed with slightly larger bodies by Robin Hood Bodyworks in Hampshire. The competition started in late June 1987, after Badgerline had been advised that their bid to buy Wilts & Dorset had been unsuccessful.

Badgerline's base for Salisbury was at Westonian Commercials in Netherhampton where a redundant Bristol RELL was used as office and crew room. This vehicle, previously a two-door Bristol City bus, was known as the 'battle wagon' due to its resemblance to a tank and its purpose.

A further attack on the Company occurred when Badgerline joined forces with Southern Vectis, another unsuccessful bidder, to form Badger Vectis. This company was to run services in Wilts & Dorset's southern area around Poole. This time a different operating strategy was used. Larger conventional type single- and double-deck buses were used, with conductors, in addition to minibuses. These routes came into operation at the end of September 1987 with the active support of Yellow Buses, whose garage at Mullard

Road in Bournemouth was used as a base.

Vehicles were supplied by both Badgerline and Southern Vectis for the operation and consisted of older Bristol RELLs, slightly newer Bristol VRTs, including some purchased from London Country in Bristol Omnibus days, and second-hand double-deckers originally operating in Manchester. For obvious reasons, the routes were designed to avoid competing with Yellow Buses themselves.

In the face of this intense competition, Wilts & Dorset was obliged to combat the competition in a radical way. The Directors decided to retaliate with purpose-built minibuses and after careful consideration an order was placed with MCW for 23-seat versions of their Metrorider minibus.These proved to be very acceptable to customers who preferred to travel on these rather than van-derived minibuses.

The response by Wilts & Dorset caused Badgerline and Badger Vectis to reconsider their position. The Poole operation collapsed in February 1988 and services were withdrawn without giving the required 42 days' notice of withdrawal to the Traffic Commissioners. The Salisbury routes continued until May 1988 when they too were withdrawn.

Other competitors also assumed that they would be able to take business from established Wilts & Dorset operations in the Company's southern district. Among these was Poole Bay Services who extended their Poole to Boscombe route to Christchurch. Charlie's Cars, owned by Drawlane, extended their minibus service into Poole while Yellow Buses, the transport department of Bournemouth City Council, in turn doubled the frequency of their journeys into Poole. This resulted in Wilts & Dorset launching a new service between Poole and Boscombe.

The substantial amount of money spent in this competitive environment had originally been intended for a scheduled vehicle replacement programme. This plan had to be delayed to permit the urgent purchase of minibuses in order to combat effectively the onslaught from rival operators. The 'war' in Salisbury and Poole had been a very costly business for all parties.

Since those days of fierce competition the Company has taken delivery of 75 new Metrorider minibuses and has also purchased a further 13 secondhand examples from Blackburn Transport (one),Grimsby and Cleethorpes Transport (six) and Yorkshire Rider (six) all built in 1987 by MCW with identical bodywork to those supplied to Wilts & Dorset but with minor internal differences and siting of hopper-style opening windows.

A comparison of the fleet list on the date of privatisation of the Company and the latest list graphically illustrates the extent of the modernisation which has taken place (see Appendices B & C). Optare Spectra double-deckers have dramatically improved the standards of comfort offered to the customers on the more intensive urban and interurban routes throughout the Company's territory and a number of Optare Delta single-deckers have replaced older Leyland Nationals on routes which either prevent the use of double-deckers or journeys which do not warrant the operation of larger capacity buses.

All services see a variety of vehicle types operating certain journeys, and vehicle utilisation is carefully planned by the Traffic Department to obtain the greatest efficiency in catering for the passenger demands. During the late 1970s and early 1980s the National Bus Company carried out intensive surveys under the Market Analysis Project (MAP) where every journey was surveyed at least once. This information was then fed into a computer with additional ticket machine information and a pattern of routes developed from this along demand lines effectively designed to cater for the majority of passengers. From this project a number of 'local identity' names were introduced to promote the revised networks of routes which included Wiltsway for the services in and around the Salisbury area.

Wilts & Dorset celebrated its tenth anniversary on 1 April 1993 which was commemorated by the production of an attractive booklet published jointly with The Wessex Transport Society.

A large number of MCW Metrorider 23-seater minibuses were taken into stock to combat competition during 1987 to 1989. These were, and continue to be, operated under the brand name Skippers. One of those received in January 1989 was No 2366 (F366 URU) which is seen at Poole Bus Station in June 1989 awaiting its next trip to Upton on Service 94. These vehicles are to be seen throughout the company's operating area on both urban routes in Poole and Salisbury and elsewhere on more rural services. (Bristol Vintage Bus Group)

Acquired from Eastern National in 1986, No 3763 (VNO 738S) is a Leyland National equipped to seat 49 passen gers with a further 24 standing and was new in October 1977. It is now allocated to the reserve fleet but is seen in 1987 during competition from Badgerline, in New Canal en-route to Salisbury's Bemerton Heath Estate on Service 54. It was still wearing NBC red livery at that time but like the rest of the fleet now carries the new Wilts & Dorset colours and fleetnames. Only overall advertisements and a very limited number of special liveries are the exception to this rule. (Bristol Vintage Bus Group)

A number of dual-purpose Leyland Nationals were bought for operating longer distance routes in Hants & Dorset days. One allocated to Wilts & Dorset in 1983 when Hants & Dorset was broken up for privatisation was No 3644 (GLJ 680N) seen here entering Poole Bus Station on Service X2 from Southampton after the route had been extended from Bournemouth to Poole in 1986. Bought by Hants & Dorset in January 1975 it has now been withdrawn from service. (Bristol Vintage Bus Group)

Leyland National No 3641 (GLJ 677N) carries the new Wilts & Dorset bus livery which is particularly attractive on these vehicles. Arriving in Bournemouth on service 123 from Lymington it has now been removed from stock (Bristol Vintage Bus Group)

One Bristol LH6L, No 3822 (REU 328S), was painted in a special livery for use on the Poole Quay Shuttle from Poole Bus Station to Poole Quay which ran between 1985 and 1987. It is seen entering Poole Bus Station with passengers from the Quay in 1985. (Bristol Vintage Bus Group)

To combat competition in Poole from Badgerline and Charlie's Cars, 15 Bristol VRTs with Metro Cammell Weymann 76-seat bodies were purchased from West Midlands Travel in 1987. New in October 1975, No 3648 (JOV 708P) is travelling along Kingland Road on 10 October 1987 approaching Poole Bus Station on Service 95. This was one of the routes introduced to combat competition at the time but which still operates, although now with Skipper minibuses. All ex-West Midlands VRTs have now been withdrawn from service. (Martin S Curtis)

Arriving in Bath in August 1989 on Service X4 from Salisbury is No 3643 (GLJ 679N). This dual-purpose Leyland National which was new in January 1975 is carrying the new style company fleetname on the white upper side panels of the old NBC dual-purpose livery. Dual-purpose Leyland Olympians, Optare Spectras and Leyland Tiger coaches have been used by Salisbury Depot on the Wilts & Dorset journeys of this joint route with Badgerline. No 3643 has now been taken out of service. (Bristol Vintage Bus Group)

Chapter Eight: Destination - The 21st Century

Determination to be the best possible and offer tangible quality at a reasonable cost is the key to success in all businesses and this principle equally applies to the provision of public transport. It is with this in mind that Wilts & Dorset looks towards the future with confidence but always fully aware that unforeseen problems or difficulties could be waiting around the corner.

Certain reasons for journeys continue basically unchanged including market day and holiday travel. Although the demand for services for both styles of travel have been affected by car ownership, markets held in the various towns and cities in the company's area, and Bank Holidays, result in extra passengers wishing to travel. The present awareness of the negative aspects of high car ownership may well result in public transport, particularly buses, returning to an element of their former importance as people movers. This has occurred where park and ride schemes have been introduced in urban areas and attempts have been made to reduce the number of cars entering cities and towns whose streets were never made to accommodate so many vehicles.

The continually changing pattern of travel needs of customers is a problem which all bus companies face and is reflected by the number of timetable amendments in any given period. Sometimes, however, these changes in demand are overcome by adjustments to the scheduled usage of buses which does not affect the published timetable. Demand for school journeys is a major problem with each new academic year particularly where a large influx of pupils who are not entitled to travel passes was not anticipated.

Effective and efficient deployment of both vehicles and staff is essential as both resources are expensive and need to be carefully planned. Inevitably, even the best made plans are thwarted on occasions but great use is made in assessing survey and electronic ticket machine data by experienced District Traffic Office staff at Poole and Salisbury.

Routes radiate from the main urban centres in the company's territory at Poole, Bournemouth and Salisbury and the smaller towns of Lymington, Swanage, Ringwood, Blandford, Romsey and Amesbury in addition to outstation sites with as few as one bus at Bowerchalke, Devizes, Downton,

Hindon, Pewsey, Porton Down, Shaftesbury and Warminster. Vehicle maintenance is carried out in the workshops of all five of the company's main depots where up-to-date equipment is available to maintain the vehicles, plant and equipment to the stringent requirement of the Company and the Department of Transport. Major maintenance, accident repairs, vehicle modification and development is carried out at the workshops in Poole and Salisbury depots whilst until recently the vehicle livery was kept pristine by using painting facilities at Blandford depot.

Vehicle maintenance and engineering performance are carefully monitored and aided by an Engineering Computer System which is installed at all of the Company's workshops and linked to the Company's Head Office at Towngate House in Poole. This comprehensive system incorporates vehicle maintenance costing, stock control, fuel and mileage monitoring.

In 1993, after its initial period of stabilisation, the Company was in a position to embark on a fleet replacement programme involving high specification Optare Spectra double-deck, Delta single-deck and MetroRider minibuses. The Company has received the largest batch of low-height Spectras supplied to any British bus operator from the Optare manufacturer based in Leeds.

At present, driver training is arranged locally at Salisbury and Poole using Bristol LH manual gearbox single-deck buses which are used on bus service work when not required on driver training duties. Acceptable applicants are trained by Relief Driving Instructors who revert to driving duties when they are not carrying out training. After their period of instruction these trainee drivers are tested by an examiner from the Driving Standards Agency, usually in either Poole or Chiseldon near Swindon. Following a day in the Conducting School new drivers then spend a period of two weeks putting into practice all that they have learnt under the supervision of a tutor driver in order to gain appropriate experience and confidence.

Unlike many other bus companies, Wilts & Dorset appoints Relief Inspectors and Engineering Supervisors who resume their normal allocated skilled engineering or driving duties when not required by the Company to carry out supervisory work. This arrangement works extremely well and offers the Company the desired flexibility of supervisory work coverage and develops individuals who successfully apply for these positions prior to full time appointment to supervisory roles.

The company has purchased other operators where it was felt to be in the company's interest. In February 1989 Verwood Transport was taken over and a Bristol VRT double-decker painted in the blue livery previously carried by Verwood Transport buses. This VRT, carrying registration number URU 691S and fleet number 4384, was still painted in this livery in August 1994.

In May 1993 a further acquisition of a PSV operator occurred when Damory Coaches based in Blandford Forum was purchased together with the vehicles and operating base in the Industrial Estate at Blandford Heights. Another expansion took place in November 1993 when the businesses of Oakfield Travel and Stanbridge & Crichel were purchased. The Oakfield unit had been running local bus services on tender to Dorset

County Council between Sturminster Newton and Blandford Forum since 1986 in addition to elements of private hire and contracts. The owners of Oakfield Travel took over Stanbridge & Crichel Bus Company in 1989 which had been operating local services in the Wimborne and Cranborne areas. All of these companies are being operated under the registrations owned by Hants & Dorset, a subsidiary of Wilts & Dorset, as autonomous units. The Oakfield garage is in Blandford while the Stanbridge & Crichel garage was based in Stanbridge itself.

As this book was in the process of being completed the business of Tourist Coaches of Figheldean near Salisbury was taken over by Wilts & Dorset Holdings Ltd on 1 February 1995 and will continue to operate with its own livery.

New technology for the years ahead is very difficult to predict but Wilts & Dorset will adapt to this and adopt the aspects that are appropriate for the continued success of the Company. Its willingness to face all kinds of challenges has been very well demonstrated to date and Wilts & Dorset can confidently face the future.

Narrow roads figure prominently on the Hindon services, well illustrated here by No 3059 (NEL 114P) negotiating Donhead St Andrew on the Service 26 journey from Shaftesbury to Hindon on 5 April 1988. A Leyland Leopard PSU3C/4R with Plaxton 49-seat coach bodywork, it was new in March 1976 and by the time that this photograph was taken had been transferred to dual-purpose status. (P Trevaskis)

The twin bores of Tisbury rail arches see No 3672 (NEL 125P), a Leyland National with 49-seat bus body, new in 1976, passing beneath the rail tracks on the Swallowcliffe Corner to Hindon journey on 11 May 1988. This vehicle has now been removed from stock. (P Trevaskis)

In January 1985 ten Leyland Tiger TL11/3RH coaches were purchased. All had Duple Laser bodywork; the first four with 51 seats for National Express work and finished in the white National Express livery, the others having 53 seats for private hire, excursion and other coaching work. Carrying the original local coach livery adapted from the NBC style is No 3205 (B205 REL). (Wilts & Dorset Bus Company Ltd)

From the 1970s onwards the advertising industry has recognised the eye-catching potential of using buses for overall advertisements. A number of Wilts & Dorset buses have been so treated including two promoting local builders merchants Sherry and Haycock. No 3425 (ELJ 217V) is seen at Cholderton on 21 May 1987 operating the Service 63 journey from Salisbury to Tidworth. This Bristol VRTSL/6G is now in the low mileage fleet, renumbered 4425 and in standard fleet livery. (P Trevaskis)

A special version of the company's livery was applied to the dual-purpose Leyland Olympians exemplified by No 3901 (A901 JPR) in Blue Boar Row, Salisbury, seen when operating to Woodfalls. These vehicles have seen extensive use on private hire and express duties and all are allocated to Salisbury Depot. This view was taken on 7 January 1995. (Brian Pike)

Three Leyland Olympians with Gardner 6LXB engines were purchased from Crosville Wales in June 1990. One was No 3923 (A175 VFM) completed with Eastern Coach Works 77-seat bodywork and non-opening front upper-deck windows which was new in May 1984. (Gerald Good)

Huge investment has been made by the company in the purchase of new vehicles since 1987. These had initially included mainly minibuses for competitive reasons but in recent years double-deck and full-size single-deck buses together with three coaches have been purchased. The first new double-deckers since the Olympians of 1984 were received in April 1993 including Optare Spectra No 3110 (K110 VLJ) with Optare 77-seat bodywork on DAF running units. It is pictured arriving at Blue Boar Row in Salisbury from Poole and Bournemouth and is based at Salisbury Depot. (Wilts & Dorset Bus Company Ltd)

Salisbury Cathedral peers over the tree tops as No 3110 (K110 VLJ) leaves the roundabout at Exeter Street on its way to Southampton on Service X7. This 77-seat bus was delivered in April 1993 as part of the initial batch of DAF/Optare Spectras for the company, being the first new double-deckers for nine years. (Wilts & Dorset Bus Company Ltd)

The absence of a rear lower-deck window is apparent in this photograph of DAF Optare Spectra No 3102 (K102 VLJ) at Organford near Lychett Minster. Later models of this vehicle incorporate a reversing camera which is positioned between the upper trafficator lights. Note the provision of numerous lights, including repeater and marker lights. (Wilts & Dorset Bus Company Ltd)

With Corfe Castle in the background Optare Spectra No 3118 (L118 ALJ) operates Service 142 between Poole and Swanage. This vehicle is allocated to Poole Depot. (Wilts & Dorset Bus Company Ltd)

Ringwood (Meeting House Lane) sees Optare Spectra No 3119 (L119 ALJ) operating from Salisbury to Bournemouth and Poole during the summer of 1994. Meeting House Lane is an important connecting point for certain Wilts & Dorset services including the X3 route and resembles a mini bus station many times each day. (Wilts & Dorset Bus Company Ltd)

Delivered during late summer of 1994, Optare Spectra No 3132 (M132 HPR) is seen here on 7 January 1995 leaving Salisbury Bus Station on Service 9 for Andover. Improvement work at Salisbury including angled departure bays and new passenger barriers can be noted in the background. Services between Salisbury and Andover are jointly operated with Hampshire Bus which is part of the Stagecoach Group. (Brian Pike)

Four 73-seat Optare Spectras have been delivered as replacements for the dual-purpose Leyland Olympians which are now over 11 years old. These Spectras have been delivered in the double-deck dual-purpose livery for use on private hire work from Salisbury Depot. The first to arrive was No 3136 (M136 KRU) seen here when operating to Bemerton Heath on Service 53 via Canadian Avenue and St Gregory's Avenue which runs hourly during the day. Since the summer of 1994, Wilts & Dorset vehicles have been fitted with yellow on black 'Dayglo' destination and numeral blinds to improve the clarity of displays for the public. This photograph was taken on 3 February 1995. (S M Chislett)

The dual-purpose livery sits extremely well on the DAF Optare Spectra double-deckers which have been fitted with 73 individual seats and numbered 3136 to 3139 (M136-139 KRU). These vehicles have replaced the 1984 Leyland Olympians on private hire work at Salisbury and the Olympians are undergoing a refurbishment programme during which the coach seats are to be replaced by bus seating. Two of these will be finished in Guide Friday livery and equipped with public address systems to replace the Series 2 Bristol VRTs from the 1995 Stonehenge Tour season. This nearside view of 3136 was taken while the bus was laying over between runs at Salisbury Garage on 8 February 1995. (S M Chislett)

National Express work commits two Wilts & Dorset vehicles to Service 005 between Yeovil, Salisbury and London (Victoria) on a contract basis between the companies. Three new Bova Futura 49-seat coaches with toilet facilities were purchased in December 1993 to replace the Leyland Tigers with Laser bodies. These new coaches entered service from January 1994. All three are posed here for a publicity shot at Wilton House on 31 December 1993 and are 3211 (L211 CRU); 3212 (L212 CRU) and 3213 (L213 CRU). All are finished in the white National Express livery required for the contract. (Wilts & Dorset Bus Company Ltd)

With the County Hotel in Bridge Street as a backdrop and the old Salisbury Infirmary clock tower by the front of the bus, Optare Delta No 3504 (L504 AJT) with Optare 48-seat body is operating to Bemerton Heath on Service 51. This estate sees double-deckers, full-size single-deckers, 23- and 31-seat Skipper minibuses at various times. Three of the six Deltas are based at Salisbury Depot and were received in the summer of 1993. (Wilts & Dorset Bus Company Ltd)

A nearside shot of Optare Delta No 3505 (L505 AJT) at Salisbury Bus Station on 7 January 1995 shows the vehicle laying over after arrival on Service 8 from Andover. These buses are to be seen on a variety of routes in the Poole and Salisbury areas. The other Deltas are based at Poole Depot (two) and Lymington Depot (one). (Brian Pike)

With the demise of the MCW manufacturing base during 1991 the Metrorider design was taken over by Optare of Leeds. Wider and longer versions seating 31 passengers arrived from March 1992 including MetroRider No 2506 (J506 RPR) seen here at Lymington Garage. (Bristol Vintage Bus Group)

Optare supplied a 29-seat MetroRider demonstrator to assist with overcoming the late delivery of vehicles to the company. L836 MWT is seen in New Canal, Salisbury operating Service 60A to Wilton via a very low railway bridge in Cherry Orchard Lane on 18 October 1994. This bus carried Optare's livery of silver and blue. (Brian Pike)

Deliveries of 31-seat Optare MetroRiders continued in late 1994 and included No 2534 (M534 JLJ) seen after arriving in Southampton (Castle Way) on Service X7 with the destination blind prepared for the return journey to Salisbury. These vehicles introduced a different body design incorporating a more upright destination box and a totally redesigned rear. In this view, taken on 4 January 1995, Solent Blue Line Olympians can be seen in the background parked up on opposite sides of the road between journeys. (Brian Pike)

Another view of No 2534 (M534 JLJ) giving the offside perspective taken in Endless Street, Salisbury when it was operating on Service 64 to Allington on 25 October 1994. (Brian Pike)

Seen at Poole Garage with its 'lid' on is No 3907 (A990 XAF) a Leyland Olympian new to North Devon (Red Bus) in April 1984 as a fixed-top bus. Purchased by Wilts & Dorset in 1986, its Eastern Coach Works 75-seat body was modified to convertible open-top for use on Service 150 between Bournemouth and Swanage via Sandbanks Ferry. A number of other second-hand Leyland Olympians were sourced from different operators for similar treatment. (Martin S Curtis)

Seen with its 'lid' off at Swanage Railway Station on 26 August 1989 is No 3909 (UWW 17X) on the right, together with No 3907 (A990 XAF). No 3909 is a Bristol Olympian formerly with West Yorkshire PTE. (Martin S Curtis)

Removal of roofs on convertible open-top
buses involves the use of a hired crane
and a number of company staff from the
Engineering Department to supervise this
delicate operation. This, until recently,
was carried out at Salisbury Garage where
3912 (EWY 80Y) is seen being so treated.
A Leyland Olympian with Roe 76-seat
convertible bodywork, it was new to West
Yorkshire PTE as a fixed-top bus in March
1983 and purchased by Wilts & Dorset in 1987
for modification to convertible open-top.
(Wilts & Dorset Bus Company Ltd)

A stack of roofs from various convertible open top Leyland Olympians is seen at Salisbury Garage. Special trolleys had been constructed specifically for the storage of these until the roofs were replaced at the end of each summer season to allow the buses to be used on other services during the winter period. (Wilts & Dorset Bus Company Ltd)

Captured with its 'lid' on is convertible open-top Leyland Olympian No 3909 (UWW 17X) which was new in March 1982 to West Yorkshire PTE as a fixed-top bus. It was acquired by Wilts & Dorset in 1987, made convertible open-top and fitted with a special suspension lift system for use over Sandbanks ferry. (Bristol Vintage Bus Group)

Each bus using the Sandbanks Ferry is equipped with special suspension units to avoid grounding when driving on or off the ferry. Vehicle No 3908 (UWW 12X) departs on the Sandbanks side of the old ferry on Service 150 for Bournemouth. A new vessel took over the operation of the ferry service in 1994. This Leyland Olympian was another bus new to West Yorkshire PTE in April 1982 which was acquired by Wilts & Dorset in early 1987 and modified to convertible open-top. (Chris Allnatt)

On 12 June 1992 Bristol VRTSL/6G No 3437 (GEL 687V), carrying an overall advertisement for Goadsby and Harding estate agents, plunged into the pedestrian subway at Fleetsbridge Round-about, Poole when operating a lunchtime journey on Service 131 from Corfe Mullen. Fortunately, there were no serious injuries to any of the twenty five passengers on the bus or pedestrians using the subway. (Evening Echo, Bournemouth)

MCW Metrorider No 2356 (F356 URU) carrying a 23-seat body was involved in an accident on 2 September 1992 resulting in the Skipper minibus turning over. The collision occurred at the Brixey Road and Rosemary Road junction in Upper Parkstone. The vehicle was returned to service after repair. Bus travel in general has an excellent safety record and serious accidents are extremely rare. Wilts & Dorset carry 18 million passengers over 10 million miles of route each year, using one and a quarter million gallons of fuel. (Evening Echo, Bournemouth)

Despite the company's best endeavours, buses do sometimes break down. If the bus cannot be moved under its own power it is towed to the nearest Wilts & Dorset garage to be repaired. Here Ford recovery lorry No 9083 (EEW 702V) is seen with a Leyland Olympian bus at St. Peter's Roundabout, Bournemouth. (Chris Allnatt)

Many bus companies adapt vehicles to perform work as breakdown trucks with specific equipment attached to suit requirements of the fleet. Salisbury Garage has a Volvo allocated for this purpose, carrying registration number XAG 222S, which is fully equipped for heavy-duty recovery. The towing and lifting gear can be seen on the back of the truck with a fuel tank for diesel replenishment in this photograph taken at Salisbury Garage on 8 February 1995. (S M Chislett)

Route maintenance is essential to reduce the amount of damage caused by trees to buses, particularly double-deckers. Lopping and pruning offending branches on trees is sometimes carried out by company staff using vehicle number 9077 (ORU 532M) which was once a standard Bristol LH6L with Eastern Coach Works 43-seat front-entrance bodywork. Originally No 3532 in the Hants & Dorset fleet and new in 1974 it has been fitted with a staircase and roof box, and converted into a tree lopper with an overall

yellow livery. Although normally allocated to Poole Depot it can be seen throughout the whole Wilts & Dorset area on tree-cutting duties and is seen here parked at Salisbury Garage. (Gerald Good)

Bristol LH6L No 3851 (AFB 587V) is used at Salisbury for driver training and is equipped with an appropriate display on the destination blind as shown in this picture taken at Salisbury Bus Station on 7 February 1995. New to Bristol Omnibus Company Ltd in 1980 it was one of a number purchased by Hants & Dorset after a very short period of time with Bristol. It carries the usual Eastern Coach Works 43-seat front-entrance body. When not required for driver training the vehicle is used on stage carriage journeys and frequently ends up overnight at Hindon outstation. (S M Chislett)

May 1990 saw the introduction of guided tours to Stonehenge as a joint venture between the company and Guide Friday, an established operator of guided tours in various cities and towns in Britain and abroad. At present two Bristol VRTSL2/6Gs are used on the summer service and 3332 (JJT 444N), now renumbered 4332, is seen at Stonehenge. New in July 1975 with 4334 (JJT 446N), they carry a special livery to promote the tour. These buses are due to be replaced with two of the 1984 Leyland Olympians following refurbishment. (Prophoto/Wilts & Dorset Bus Company Ltd)

Seen here unloading passengers at the Swanage Railway's Harmans Cross Station after arrival from Corfe Castle on a summer's day in 1992, No 4001 (XSL 228A) is a Bristol FS6G with Eastern Coach Works 60-seat body convertible for open-top operation and has a rear open platform. Originally new to Bristol Omnibus Company Ltd in 1961 and used on the open-top sea-front service in Weston-super-Mare it is known affectionately as "Nelly" and was acquired by Wilts & Dorset from Hampshire Bus in January 1992. It is painted in a special Swanage Railway livery and is used exclusively on work connected with the Swanage Railway. (Andrew Wright)

Damory Coaches No 5032 (TEL 492R) was originally Wilts & Dorset No 3726. New in July 1977, this Leyland National carries dual-purpose seating for 48 passengers and is still operating for Damory Coaches. Seen here at picturesque Milton Abbas it is operating on Service 311 between Blandford and Dorchester in 1994. (Damory Coaches)

Pictured at the Tourist Coaches depot at Figheldean in January 1995, B873 XWR is a Volvo B10M-61 coach with Plaxton 53-seat bodywork which was new in 1985. Beside it is YPD 124Y, a Leyland TRCTL11/2R coach with a Duple 53-seat body new in May 1983. In the background HSV 342, a MAN SR280 coach with a MAN 48-seat toilet-fitted body can be glimpsed. This vehicle was new in November 1981 when it was registered KMR 3X. (Tourist Coaches)

As a result of the takeover of the Oakfield and Stanbridge and Crichel businesses to form Damory Coaches, a number of vehicles were transferred from Wilts & Dorset to upgrade the fleet. A vehicle making the opposite move to join the Wilts & Dorset fleet at Salisbury was No 3278 (B278 KPF), a 1984 Leyland Tiger with Plaxton 53-seat bodywork. The dual-purpose livery suits the body style well. (S M Chislett)

HAIL-A-BUS USERS' CODE

Nearly everyone likes the convenience of HAIL-A-BUS. We like it too.
But it is now so popular that we need your help to keep everyone happy.

If you remember these **three** points, that will help us to keep HAIL-A-BUS running smoothly.

1 Let the driver know in good time when you want the bus to stop

2 Bear in mind that the driver can only stop where it is safe for people to get on or off the bus and for other vehicles on the road

3 Remember that your stop is your fellow passengers' delay. If near neighbours could get on or off at the same point, the bus won't have to stop too often in a short distance

WILTS & DORSET
Help us to help you

Appendix A: Wilts & Dorset Fleetlist as at December 1965

Depots: Salisbury, Basingstoke, Blandford, Andover, Amesbury and Pewsey, with outstations at Bowerchalke, Hindon, Ringwood, Romsey, Shaftesbury and Warminster.

301-313 Bristol K5G; ECW   L55R Built 1950

301 GHR 365	302 GHR 366	303 GHR 367
304 GHR 368	311 GMR 26	312 GMR 27
313 GMR 28		

314-320 Bristol KS6B(*KS5G); ECW L55R Built 1950

314 GMR 893	315 GMR 894	316 GMW 194
317 GMW 195	318 GMW 196	320*GMW 851

321-323 Bristol LL6B; ECW   B39R Built 1950

321 GMW 911	322 GMW 912	323 GMW 913

---

324   Bristol KS5G; ECW   L55R Built 1951

324 GWV 305		

325-378 Bristol KSW5G; ECW   L55R Built 1951-53

325 GWV 929	326 HAM 229	327 HAM 230
328 HAM 231	329 HAM 693	330 HAM 694
331 HAM 695	332 HAM 696	333 HHR 60
334 HHR 61	335 HHR 62	336 HHR 63
337 HHR 64	338 HHR 750	340 HHR 822
341 HHR 823	342 HMR 12	343 HMR 58
344 HMR 59	345 HMR 414	346 HMR 415
347 HMR 416	348 HMR 624	349 HMR 688
350 HMR 689	351 HMR 690	352 HMR 743
353 HMR 744	354 HMR 745	355 HMR 746
356 HMR 747	357 HMR 809	358 HMR 810
359 HMW 445	360 HMW 446	361 HMW 447
362 HMW 448	363 HWV 292	364 HWV 293
365 HWV 294	366 JAM 419	367 JAM 420
368 JAM 933	369 JHR 140	370 JHR 141
371 JHR 142	372 JHR 883	373 JHR 959
374 JHR 960	375 JMW 243	376 JMW 317
377 JMW 499	378 JMW 955	

379-393 Bristol KSW6B; ECW   L55RD Built 1953

379 JMW 954	380 JWV 263	381 JWV 380
382 JWV 381	383 JWV 382	384 JWV 383
385 JWV 849	386 JWV 978	387 JWV 979
388 KAM 594	389 KAM 595	390 KHR 103
391 KHR 104	392 KHR 529	393 KHR 530

516-552 Bristol LS6G; ECW DP39/41F(*B41F)Built 1952-54

516 HWV 944	517 HWV 945	518 HWV946
519 JAM 151	520 JAM 152	521 JAM225
522 JAM 226	523 JAM 227	524 JAM303
525 JAM 304	526 JAM 305	527 JAM306
528 JAM 418	529 JHR 388	530 JHR389
531 JHR 494	532 JHR 495	533 JHR604
534 JHR 605	535 JMR 13	536 JMR85
537 JMR 86	538 JMR 323	539 JMR324
540 JMR 325	541 JMR 637	542 JMR638
543 JMR 639	544 JMW 412	545 JMW 413
546 JMW 669	547 JMW 670	548 JWV 261
549 JWV 262	550*JWV 761 551*JWV 762 552*KHR 654	

553-567 Bristol LWL5G; ECW   FB39F Built 1954

553 KWV 933	554 KWV 934	555 KWV 935
556 KWV 936	557 LAM 107	558 LAM 108
559 LAM 109	560 LAM 110	561 LAM 278
562 LAM 465	563 LAM 743	564 LAM 744
565 LAM 745	566 LHR 857	567 LHR 858

568-592 Bristol LS5G; ECW   B41F Built 1955-56

568 LWV 844	569 LWV 845	570 LWV 846
571 LWV 847	572 LWV 848	573 LWV 964
574 LWV 965	575 LWV 966	576 NAM 116
577 NAM 117	578 NAM 286	579 NAM 287
580 NAM 288	581 NHR 128	582 NHR 129
583 NHR 723	584 OAM 125	585 OAM 366
586 OAM 367	587 OAM 552	588 OAM 553
589 OHR 389	590 OHR 390	591 OHR 587
592 OMR 56		

600-605 Bristol LD6G; ECW   LD58R Built 1954

600 KMR 608	601 KMR 609	602 KMW 109
603 KMW 345	604 KMW 916	605 KMW 917

606-613 Bristol LD6B; ECW   LD58R Built 1954-5

606 LMR 155	607 LMR 740	608 LMR 741
609 LMR 742	610 LMW 680	611 LMW 914
612 LMW 915	613 LMW 916	

614-637 Bristol LD6G(*LD6B); ECW   LD60R(+LD60RD)
Built 1955-59

614*MMW 411	615*MMW 412	616*MMW 413
617*+NHR 844	618*+NHR 845	619*+NHR 909
620+OAM 969	621+OHR 57	622+OHR 123
623+OHR 124	624 OHR 382	625 OHR 509
626 OHR 708	627 OHR 709	628 OHR 919
629 OHR 918	630+PMR 913	631+PMR 914
632+PWV 353	633+RWV 526	634+SHR 440
635+SHR 441	636+TMW 273	637+UAM 941

638-650 Bristol FS6G(*FS6B); ECW LD60RD Built 1962

638 676 AAM	639 677 AAM	640 678 AAM
641 679 AAM	642 680 AAM	643 681 AAM
644 682 AAM	645 683 AAM	646 684 AAM
647 685 AAM	648*686 AAM	649*687 AAM
650*688 AAM		

651-657 Bristol FS6B; ECW   LD60R Built 1963

651 689 AAM	652 690 AAM	653 691 AAM
654 692 AAM	655 693 AAM	656 694 AAM
657 695 AAM		

658-663 Bristol FLF6G; ECW   LD70F Built 1963-64

658 467 BMR	659 468 BMR	660 469 BMR
661 470 BMR	662 AHR 244B	663 AHR 246B

664-671 Bristol FS6B; ECW   LD60RD Built 1963/64
664 473 BMR   665 474 BMR   666 475 BMR
667 476 BMR   668 477 BMR   669 478 BMR
670 479 BMR   671 AHR 245B

701-720 Bristol MW6G; ECW   C39F   Built 1958-62
     (* are 31 feet long)
701 RHR 852   702 RHR 853   703 RMR 542
704 RMR 736   705 RMR 992   706 RMR 995
707 SWV 688   708 SWV 689   709 XMR 942
710 XMR 943   711 XMR 944   712 XMR 945
713 XMR 946   714 XMR 947   715 673 AAM
716 674 AAM   717 675 AAM   718*130 AMW
719*131 AMW   720*132 AMW

721-722 Bristol MW6G; ECW   DP41F Built 1963
721 133 AMW   722 134 AMW

801-810 Bristol MW6G; ECW   B43F Built 1961-2
801 XMR 948   802 XMR 949   803 XMR 950
804 XMR 951   805 XMR 952   806 XMR 953
807 XMR 954   808 XMR 955   809 XMR 956
810 XMR 957

901-903 Leyland Tiger Cub PSUC1/2; Harrington   DP41F
    Built 1957-58, ex Silver Star in 1963 (Nos 31-33)
901 PHR 829   902 PMW 386   903 RAM 620

904   Leyland Royal Tiger PSU1/15; Harrington   C41C
     Chassis built 1953; Body built 1956,
     ex Silver Star No 28 in 1963
904 HWV 793

905-907 Leyland Tiger Cub PSUC1/2; Harrington C41F(*DP41F)
     Built 1956/58, ex Silver Star Nos 29, 30 and 34 in 1963
905 OHR 280   906 OHR 281   907*SAM 47

908-909 Leyland Leopard L2; Harrington   C41F   Built 1960
     ex Silver Star Nos 38 and 39 in 1963
908 WAM 441   909 WWV 564

910-914 Bedford SB13; Duple   C41F   Built 1965
910 BMW 135C   911 BMW 136C   912 BMW 137C
913 BMW 138C   914 BMW 139C

BODY CODES (before seating capacity)
B Single-deck bus   C Single-deck coach
F Full front   DP Dual-purpose single-decker
L Lowbridge double-deck bus with sunken upper deck gangway
LD Lowheight double-deck bus with central upper deck gangway

BODY CODES (after seating capacity)
C Central entrance   F Front entrance
R Rear entrance (open platform)
RD Rear entrance with platform doors

Light figures denote a.m. times.   Dark figures denote p.m. times.

Service 10 — SALISBURY—UPAVON—DEVIZES — DAILY

	S	M-F	NSu*	NSu*	C*	NSu	NSu	NSu										
Salisbury, Bus Station	—	—	6-5	6-45	7-45	8-50	9-50	10-50	11-50	12-50	1-50	2-50	3-50	4-50	5-50	6-50	7-50	8-50
Amesbury, Bus Station	6-15	6-20	6-25	7-10	8-10	9-10	10-10	11-10	12-10	1-10	2-10	3-10	4-10	5-10	6-10	7-10	8-10	9-10
Stonehenge Inn	6-21	6-26	6-31	7-16	8-16	9-16	10-16	11-16	12-16	1-16	2-16	3-16	4-16	5-16	6-16	7-16	8-16	9-16
Durrington, Post Office			6-36	7-21	8-21	9-21	10-21	11-21	12-21	1-21	2-21	3-21	4-21	5-21	6-21	7-21	8-21	9-21
Netheravon, Post Office	6-35	6-40	6-45	7-30	8-30	9-30	10-30	11-30	12-30	1-30	2-30	3-30	4-30	5-30	6-30	7-30	8-30	9-30
Enford, Bus Shelter			6-52	7-37	8-37	9-37	10-37	11-37	12-37	1-37	2-37	3-37	4-37	5-37	6-37	7-37	8-37	9-37
UPAVON, Ship Inn			7-0	7-45	8-45	9-45	10-45	11-45	12-45	1-45	2-45	3-45	4-45	5-45	6-45	7-45	8-45	9-45
Charlton, Cat Inn			7-5	7-50	8-50	9-50	10-50	11-50	12-50	1-50	2-50	3-50	4-50	5-50	6-50	7-50	8-50	9-50
Wilsford Turning			7-9	7-54	8-54	9-54	10-54	11-54	12-54	1-54	2-54	3-54	4-54	5-54	6-54	7-54	8-54	9-54
Chirton, New Inn			7-15	8-0	9-0	10-0	11-0	12-0	1-0	2-0	3-0	4-0	5-0	6-0	7-0	8-0	9-0	10-0
Lydeway, Foxley Corner			7-20	8-5	9-5	10-5	11-5	12-5	1-5	2-5	3-5	4-5	5-5	6-5	7-5	8-5	9-5	10-5
Nursteed			7-29	8-14	9-14	10-14	11-14	12-14	1-14	2-14	3-14	4-14	5-14	6-14	7-14	8-14	9-14	10-14
Devizes, Market			7-35	8-20	9-20	10-20	11-20	12-20	1-20	2-20	3-20	4-20	5-20	6-20	7-20	8-20	9-20	10-20

	M-F	S	M-F	NSu	NSu	NSu	NSu											
Devizes, Market				7-40	8-40	9-40	10-40	11-40	12-40	1-40	2-40	3-40	4-40	5-40	6-40	7-40	8-40	9-40	10-25
Nursteed				7-46	8-46	9-46	10-46	11-46	12-46	1-46	2-46	3-46	4-46	5-46	6-46	7-46	8-46	9-46	10-31
Lydeway, Foxley Corner				7-55	8-55	9-55	10-55	11-55	12-55	1-55	2-55	3-55	4-55	5-55	6-55	7-55	8-55	9-55	10-40
Chirton, New Inn				8-0	9-0	10-0	11-0	12-0	1-0	2-0	3-0	4-0	5-0	6-0	7-0	8-0	9-0	10-0	10-45
Wilsford Turning				8-6	9-6	10-6	11-6	12-6	1-6	2-6	3-6	4-6	5-6	6-6	7-6	8-6	9-6	10-6	10-51
Charlton, Cat Inn			*	8-10	9-10	10-10	11-10	12-10	1-10	2-10	3-10	4-10	5-10	6-10	7-10	8-10	9-10	10-10	10-55
UPAVON, Ship Inn			†	8-15	9-15	10-15	11-15	12-15	1-15	2-15	3-15	4-15	5-15	6-15	7-15	8-15	9-15	10-15	11-0
Enford, Bus Shelter				8-23	9-23	10-23	11-23	12-23	1-23	2-23	3-23	4-23	5-23	6-23	7-23	8-23	9-23	10-23	11-8
Netheravon, Post Office		6-40	6-45	8-30	9-30	10-30	11-30	12-30	1-30	2-30	3-30	4-30	5-30	6-30	7-30	8-30	9-30	10-30	11-15
Durrington, Post Office	6-35	6-49	6-54	8-39	9-39	10-39	11-39	12-39	1-39	2-39	3-39	4-39	5-39	6-39	7-39	8-39	9-39	10-39	11-24
Stonehenge Inn	6-40	6-53	6-58	8-44	9-44	10-44	11-44	12-44	1-44	2-44	3-44	4-44	5-44	6-44	7-44	8-44	9-44	10-44	11-29
Amesbury, Bus Station	6-47	7-0	7-5	8-50	9-50	10-50	11-50	12-50	1-50	2-50	3-50	4-50	5-50	6-50	7-50	8-50	9-50	10-50	11-35
Salisbury, Bus Station	7-7	7-23	7-25	9-10	10-10	11-10	12-10	1-10	1-10	2-10	3-10	4-10	5-10	6-10	7-10	8-10	9-10	10-10	—

NSu—Not on Sundays.   *—Change at Amesbury.   C—Service commences from Amesbury only at 8-10 a.m. on Sundays.
   S—Saturdays only.   M-F—Mondays to Fridays.   †—Starts from Netheravon New Buildings.
See Service 5 for additional services between Salisbury and Upavon.

Appendix B: Wilts & Dorset Fleetlist as at 1 April 1983

Depots: Poole, Salisbury, Lymington, Blandford, Pewsey, Swanage and Ringwood with outstations at Amesbury, Romsey, Warminster, Shaftesbury, Devizes, Porton Down, Fordingbridge and Hindon.

601-630 Bristol RELL6G;ECW	B45D plus 23 standing	
Built 1969-72	* DP50F plus 23 standing	
601 MMW 351G	602 MMW 352G	604 MMW 354G
605*MMW 355G	606*MMW 356G	607*MMW 357G
609 PRU 64G	612 RLJ 798H	613 RLJ 799H
617*TRU 944J	620*TRU 947J	621*TRU 948J
622*XLJ 727K	623*XLJ 728K	624*XLJ 729K
627 CRU 137L	630 CRU 140L	

1604-1649 Bristol RELL6G;ECW	B45D plus 23 standing	
Built 1968-72	* DP50F plus 23 standing	
1604 NLJ 819G	1608 NLJ 823G	1611 NLJ 826G
1615* NLJ 871G	1616* NLJ 872G	1617 PLJ 742G
1618 PLJ 743G	1619 PLJ 744G	1620 PLJ 745G
1622 RLJ 341H	1624 RLJ 343H	1625 RLJ 344H
1626 RLJ 345H	1627 RLJ 346H	1629 RLJ 348H
1630 RLJ 349H	1632 SRU 830H	1635 TRU 217J
1636 TRU 218J	1638 UEL 558J	1639 UEL 559J
1640 UEL 560J	1641 UEL 561J	1645* UEL 565J
1646* UEL 566J	1647* XLJ 722K	1648* XLJ 723K
1649* XLJ 724K		

1901-1906 Daimler Fleetline CRG6;Roe H43/31F		Built 1971
1901 VRU 124J	1902 VRU 125J	1903 VRU 126J
1904 VRU 127J	1905 VRU 128J	1906 VRU 129J

1907-1916 Leyland Fleetline FE30;MCW		H44/32F
Built 1976-77, ex London Transport in 1983		
1907 OUC 45R	1908 OJD 179R	1909 OJD 191R
1910 OJD 193R	1911 OJD 217R	1912 OJD 190R
1913 OJD 225R	1914 OJD 230R	1915 OJD 231R
1916 OJD 242R		

3307-3334 Bristol VRTSL/2 6G; ECW H43/31F Built 1974-75		
3307 NRU 307M	3309 NRU 309M	3311 NRU 311M
3324 JJT 436N	3325 JJT 437N	3326 JJT 438N
3327 JJT 439N	3328 JJT 440N	3329 JJT 441N
3330 JJT 442N	3331 JJT 443N	3332 JJT 444N
3333 JJT 445N	3334 JJT 446N	

3335-3356 Bristol VRTSL/3 6G; ECW H43/31F		Built 1976
3335 MEL 556P	3336 MEL 557P	3337 MEL 558P
3338 MEL 559P	3339 MEL 560P	3340 MEL 561P
3341 MEL 562P	3348 NJT 34P	3349 NJT 35P

3350-3356 Bristol VRTSL/3 6L(501); ECW H43/31F Built 1976		
3350 OEL 231P	3351 OEL 232P	3352 OEL 233P
3353 OEL 234P	3354 OEL 235P	3355 OEL 236P
3356 OEL 237P		

3367-3456 Bristol VRTSL/3 6G; ECW H43/31F Built 1977-80		
3367 RJT 158R	3368 RJT 159R	3380 URU 687S
3381 URU 688S	3382 URU 689S	3383 URU 690S
3384 URU 691S	3385 VPR 484S	3386 VPR 485S
3398 YEL 5T	3399 YEL 371T	3400 BFX 568T
3401 BFX 569T	3402 BFX 570T	3403 BFX 571T
3404 BFX 572T	3405 BFX 573T	3406 BFX 574T
3407 BFX 575T	3411 BFX 664T	3412 BFX 665T
3413 BFX 666T	3414 UDL 671S	3415 UDL 672S
3416 UDL 673S	3417 UDL 674S	3418 UDL 675S
3419 UDL 676S	3422 ELJ 214V	3423 ELJ 215V
3424 ELJ 216V	3425 ELJ 217V	3426 ELJ 218V
3427 ELJ 219V	3428 ELJ 220V	3429 GEL 679V
3430 GEL 680V	3431 GEL 681V	3432 GEL 682V
3433 GEL 683V	3435 GEL 685V	3436 GEL 686V
3437 GEL 687V	3448 KRU 848W	3449 KRU 849W
3450 KRU 850W	3451 KRU 851W	3453 KRU 853W
3454 KRU 854W	3455 KRU 855W	3456 KRU 856W

3608-3677 Leyland National	B49F plus 24 standing	
Built 1973-76	*DP48F plus 21 standing	
3608 NEL 851M	3610 NEL 853M	3611 NEL 854M
3612 NEL 855M	3613 NEL 856M	3619 NEL 862M
3621 NEL 864M	3628 SEL 236N	3640*GLJ 676N
3641*GLJ 677N	3642*GLJ 678N	3643*GLJ 679N
3644*GLJ 680N	3645*GLJ 681N	3646*GLJ 682N
3653 MEL 551P	3654 MEL 552P	3662 MLJ 918P
3663 MLJ 919P	3665 MLJ 921P	3672 NEL 125P
3673 NEL 126P	3674 NEL 127P	3675 NEL 128P
3676 NEL 129P	3677 NEL 130P	

3678-3751 Leyland National	B49F plus 24 standing	
	*DP48F plus 21 standing	
	+B41F plus 20 standing	
3678+PJT 255R	3679+PJT 256R	3680+PJT 257R
3681+PJT 258R	3682+PJT 259R	3695 PJT 272R
3696 PJT 273R	3702 RJT 150R	3717 VFX 983S
3721 VFX 987S	3722 VFX 988S	3726*TEL 492R
3727*TEL 493R	3730*WFX 255S	3736 XFX 897S
3737 XFX 898S	3738 BEL 730T	3739 BEL 731T
3740 BEL 732T	3744 EEL 894V	3745 FPR 61V
3750 FPR 66V	3751 FPR 67V	

3809-3858 Bristol LH6L/ECW	B43F plus 12 standing	
	Built 1975-80; all except 3809	
	ex Bristol Omnibus Company	
3809 LJT 942P	3822 REU 328S	3823 REU 329S
3825 REU 331S	3827 TTC 786T	3829 TTC 788T
3833 WAE 190T	3841 YAE 513V	3842 YAE 514V
3843 YAE 515V	3848 YAE 520V	3849 AFB 585V
3851 AFB 587V	3852 AFB 588V	3854 AFB 590V
3855 AFB 591V	3856 AFB 592V	3858 AFB 595V

BODY CODES (before seating capacity)

B Single-deck bus   DP Dual-purpose single-decker

H Double-deck bus with central upper deck gangway.

All Bristol VRTs are lowheight versions.

BODY CODES (after seating capacity)

F Front entrance   D Front entrance/central exit

Appendix C: Wilts & Dorset Fleetlist as at March 1995

Depots: Poole, Salisbury (including outstations at Amesbury, Bowerchalke, Devizes, Downton, Hindon, Pewsey, Porton Down, Ringwood, Romsey, Shaftesbury and Warminster), Ringwood, Blandford (including Shaftesbury outstation), Lymington (including outstations at Hythe and Lyndhurst) and Swanage

2301-2321	MCW MF150/47	B23F	Delivered 1987
2301 E452 MEL	2302 E453 MEL	2303 E454 MEL	
2304 E455 MEL	2305 E456 MEL	2306 E457 MEL	
2307 E458 MEL	2308 E459 MEL	2309 E460 MEL	
2310 E461 MEL	2311 E462 MEL	2312 E463 MEL	
2313 E464 MEL	2314 E465 MEL	2315 E466 MEL	
2316 E467 MEL	2317 E468 MEL	2318 E469 MEL	
2319 E470 MEL	2320 E471 MEL	2321 E472 MEL	

2322-2325	MCW MF150/48	B23F	Delivered 1987
2322 E473 MEL	2323 1 SAR (previously E474 MEL)		
2324 E475 MEL	2325 E476 MEL		

2326-2334	MCW MF150/49	B23F	Delivered 1987
2326 E477 MEL	2327 E478 MEL	2328 E479 MEL	
2329 E480 MEL	2330 E481 MEL	2331 E482 MEL	
2332 E483 MEL	2333 E484 MEL	2334 E485 MEL	

2335-2341	MCW MF150/49	B23F	Delivered 1987
2335 E486 MEL	2336 E487 MEL	2337 E488 MEL	
2338 E489 MEL	2339 E490 MEL	2340 E491 MEL	
2341 E492 MEL			

2342-2345	MCW MF150/64	B23F	Delivered 1987
2342 E493 MEL	2343 E494 MEL	2344 E495 MEL	
2345 E496 MEL			

2346-2350	MCW MF150/66	B23F	Delivered 1988
2346 E346 REL	2347 E347 REL	2348 E348 REL	
2349 E349 REL	2350 E350 REL		

2351-2365	MCW MF150/108	B23F	Delivered 1989
2351 F351 URU	2352 F352 URU	2353 F353 URU	
2354 F354 URU	2355 F355 URU	2356 F356 URU	
2357 F357 URU	2358 F358 URU	2359 F359 URU	
2362 F362 URU	2363 F363 URU	2364 F364 URU	
2365 F365 URU			

2366-2375	MCW MF150/108	B23F	Delivered 1989
2366 F366 URU	2367 F367 URU	2368 F368 URU	
2369 F369 URU	2370 F370 URU	2374 F374 URU	
2375 F375 URU			

2376	MCW MF150/42	B23F	Built 1987
	ex Blackburn 3/91		
2376 F613 FRN			

2377-2382	MCW MF150/94	B23F	Built 1988
	2377/8/80 ex Grimsby Cleethorpes 7/91		
	2379/81/2 ex Maidstone 7/91		
2377 E43 HFE	2378 E44 HFE	2379 E52 HFE	
2380 E53 HFE	2381 E54 HFE	2382 E55 HFE	

2383-2388	MCW MF150/41	B23F	Built 1987
	2383-6 ex Yorkshire Rider 8/91		
	2387-8 ex Yorkshire Rider 1/92		
2383 E227 PWY	2384 E228 PWY	2385 E229 PWY	
2386 E230 PWY	2387 E226 PWY	2388 E233 PWY	

2501-2541	Optare MR05 (2501-33) B31F Delivered 1992-3
	Optare MR15 (2534-41) B31F Delivered 1994-5
	Vehicles with the suffix F are adapted for use on
	the Sandbanks Ferry

2501 J501 RPR	2502 J502 RPR	2503 J503 RPR
2504 J504 RPR	2505 J505 RPR	2506 J506 RPR
2507 J507 RPR	2508 J508 RPR	2509 J509 RPR
2510 J510 RPR	2511 J511 RPR	2512 J512 RPR
2513 J513 RPR	2514 J514 RPR	2515 J515 RPR
2516 K516 UJT	2517 K517 UJT	2518 K518 UJT
2519 K519 UJT	2520 K520 UJT	2521 K521 UJT
2522 K522 UJT	2523 K523 UJT	2524 K524 UJT
2525 K525 UJT	2526 K526 UJT	2527 K527 UJT
2528F K528 UJT	2529F K529 UJT	2530F K530 UJT
2531F K531 UJT	2532F K532 UJT	2533F K533 UJT
2534 M534 JLJ	2535 M535 JLJ	2536 M536 JLJ
2537 M537 JLJ	2538 M538 LEL	2539 M539 LEL
2540 M540 LEL	2541 M541 LEL	

3101-3135	DAF DB250; Optare H48/29F Delivered 1993-4

3101 K101 VLJ	3102 K102 VLJ	3103 K103 VLJ
3104 K104 VLJ	3105 K105 VLJ	3106 K106 VLJ
3107 K107 VLJ	3108 K108 VLJ	3109 K109 VLJ
3110 K110 VLJ	3111 L711 ALJ	3112 L112 ALJ
3113 L113 ALJ	3114 L114 ALJ	3115 L115 ALJ
3116 L116 ALJ	3117 L117 ALJ	3118 L118 ALJ
3119 L119 ALJ	3120 L120 ALJ	3121 L121 ELJ
3122 L122 ELJ	3123 L123 ELJ	3124 L124 ELJ
3125 L125 ELJ	3126 L126 ELJ	3127 L127 ELJ
3128 L128 ELJ	3129 L129 ELJ	3130 L130 ELJ
3131 L131 ELJ	3132 M132 HPR	3133 M133 HPR
3134 M134 HPR	3135 M135 HPR	

3136-3139	DAF DB250; Optare H45/28F Delivered 1994-5
3136 M136 KRU	3137 M137 KRU	3138 M138 KRU
3139 M139 KRU		

3140-3147	DAF DB250; Optare H48/29F Delivered 1995
3140 M140 KRU	3141 M141 KRU	3142 M142 KRU
3143 M143 KRU	3144 M144 KRU	3145 M145 KRU
3144 M144 KRU	3145 M145 KRU	3146 M146 KRU
3147 M947 KRU		

3205-3210 Leyland TRCTL11/3RH; Duple C53F Delivered 1984
3205 B205 REL	3206 B206 REL	3207 B207 REL
3208 B208 REL	3209 B209 REL	3210 B210 REL

3211-3213	Bova FLD 12-270	C49FT Delivered 1993
3211 L211 CRU	3212 L212 CRU	3213 L213 CRU

3278   Leyland TRCTL11/3RH; Plaxton   C53F
Built 1985; ex Damory Coaches 1/94
3278 B278 KPF

4326-4334   Bristol VRT/SL2/6LX; ECW   H43/31F
Delivered 1975

4326 JJT 438N	4327 JJT 439N	4328 JJT 440N
4332 JJT 444N	4334 JJT 446N	

4336   Bristol VRT/SL3/6LX; ECW   H43/31F
Delivered 1976
4336 MEL 557P

3351-3353   Bristol VRT'SL3/501; ECW   3351 O43/31F
Delivered 1976   3353 H43/31F

3351 OEL 232P	3353 OEL 234P

4367-4413   Bristol VRT/SL3/6LXB; ECW   H43/31F
Delivered 1977-9

4367 RJT 158R	4368 RJT 159R	3381 URU 688S
4382 URU 689S	4383 URU 690S	4384 URU 691S
4398 YEL 5T	4399 YEL 371T	3400 BFX 568T
3401 BFX 569T	4403 BFX 571T	4404 BFX 572T
4405 BFX 573T	4406 BFX 574T	4407 BFX 575T
4411 BFX 664T	4412 BFX 665T	4413 BFX 666T

4414-4419   Bristol VRT/SL3/6LXB; ECW   H43/31F
Built 1978; ex Southern Vectis 4/79

4414 UDL 671S	3415 UDL 672S	3416 UDL 673S
4417 UDL 674S	3418 UDL 675S	4419 UDL 676S

4422-3456   Bristol VRT/SL3/6LXB; ECW   H43/31F
Delivered 1979-80

4422 ELJ 214V	4423 ELJ 215V	4424 ELJ 216V
4425 ELJ 217V	4426 ELJ 218V	4427 ELJ 219V
4428 ELJ 220V	3429 GEL 679V	4430 GEL 680V
4431 GEL 681V	4432 GEL 682V	4433 GEL 683V
3435 GEL 685V	3436 GEL 686V	4437 GEL 687V
4448 KRU 848W	3449 KRU 849W	4450 KRU 850W
4451 KRU 851W	3453 KRU 853W	3454 KRU 854W
4455 KRU 855W	3456 KRU 856W	

3457-3459   Bristol VRT/SL3/6LXB; ECW   H43/31F
Built 1979-80; ex Keighley District

3457 NUM 340V	3458 JWT 756V	3459 JWT 759V

3501-3506   DAF SB220; Optare   B48F   Delivered 1993

3501 L501 AJT	3502 L502 AJT	3503 L503 AJT
3504 L504 AJT	3505 L505 AJT	3506 L506 AJT

4722-3751   Leyland National 11351A/1R   B49F
Delivered 1978-9

4722 VFX 988S	3736 XFX 897S	3738 BEL 730T
3740 BEL 732T	3744 EEL 894V	3745 FPR 61V
3751 FPR 67V		

3763   Leyland National 11351A/1R   B49F
Built 1977; ex Eastern National 10/86
3763 VNO 738S

4833-3858   Leyland National 11351A/1R   B49F
Built 1979-80; ex Bristol Omnibus

4833 WAE 190T	3849 AFB 585V	3851 AFB 587V
3852 AFB 588V	3854 AFB 590V	3856 AFB 592V
3858 AFB 595V		

3901-3905   Leyland ONLXB/1R; ECW   H45/32F
Delivered 1984

3901 A901 JPR	3902 A902 JPR	3903 A903 JPR
3904 A904 JPR	3905 A905 JPR	

3906-3907   Leyland ONLXB/1R; ECW   CO45/30F
Built 1984; ex North Devon 6/86;
adapted for use on the Sandbanks Ferry

3906 A989 XAF	3907 A990 XAF

3908-3912   Leyland ONLXB/1R; Roe   CO47/29F
Built 1982-3; ex West Yorkshire PTE 6/87
adapted for use on the Sandbanks Ferry

3908 UWW 12X	3909 UWW 17X	4910 CUB 67Y
3911 CUB 70Y	3912 EWW 80Y	

4913   Leyland ONLXB/1R; Roe   H47/29F
Built 1982; ex Metrobus 1/89
4913 UWW 16X

3914-3920   Leyland ONTL11/1R; Roe   H43/29F
Built 1983-4; ex County Bus 6/90

3914 A144 DPE	3915 A145 DPE	3916 A156 FPG
3918 A158 FPG	3919 A159 FPG	3920 A160 FPG

3921-3923   Leyland ONLXB/1R; ECW   H45/32F
Built 1984; ex Crosville Wales 6/90

3921 A173 VFM	3922 A174 VFM	3923 A175 VFM

4924-3926   Leyland ONLXB/1R; East Lancs   H43/31F
Built 1982; ex Stevensons 12/90

4924 TTT 172X	4925 TTT 173X	3926 TTT 174X

4927   Leyland ONLXB/1R; Roe   H47/29F
Built 1982; ex Stevensons 3/91
4927 UWW 6X

4001   Bristol FS6G; ECW   CO33/27R
Built 1961; ex Bristol Omnibus (Reg 866 NHT)
and Hampshire Bus 1/92
4001 XSL 228A

BODY CODES - see the bottom of page 127
For double-deck buses the upper-deck seating capacity is shown
first, followed by the lower-deck seating capacity (eg. H48/29F)

Certain Wilts & Dorset vehicles are classified as 'low mileage'
stock and are identified by the first digit of the fleet number
becoming 4 (eg. 3448 becomes 4448)

Damory Coaches
Depots: Blandford Heights Industrial Estate and Sunrise Park, Blandford

5001	Leyland TRCTL11/3R; Plaxton	C50F
	Built 1982; ex Johnsons 8/93	
5001 SMY 635X		

5003-5006	Leyland TRCTL11/3RH; Duple	C51F
	Built 1984; ex Wilts & Dorset 1/94	

5003 701 GOO (previously B201 REL)   5005 B203 REL
5004 VUV 246 (previously B202 REL)   5006 B204 REL

5011-5015	Leyland PSU3E/4R; Plaxton	C49F
	Built 1976/7/9; ex Wilts & Dorset 11/93	

5011 NEL 114P   5013 SRU 147R   5015 BJT 323T

5014	Leyland PSU3E/4R; Duple	C49F
	Built 1979; ex Oakfield Travel 11/93	
5014 BKJ 151T		

5016-5017	Leyland PSU3G/4R; Plaxton	C51F
	Built 1981; ex Johnsons 11/93	

5016 HJB 467W   5017 HJB 470W

5025	Bedford YMT; Duple	C53F
	Built 1982; ex Kimber 5/93	
5025 DCA 523X		

5024-5026	Bedford YNT; Duple	C53F
	Built 1981-2;	
	ex Kimber 5/93(5024) and Oakfield Travel 11/93	

5024 OAL 788W   5026 XHR 748A (previously RNN 11X)

5032-5034	Leyland National 11351A/1R	5032/3 DP48F
	Built 1977/8/9;	5034 B49F
	ex Wilts & Dorset 11/93 (5032/3) and 10/94(5034)	

5032 TEL 492R   5033 WFX 255S   5034 BEL 731T

5042-5043	Bristol LH6L; ECW	B43F	Built 1979/80
	ex Wilts & Dorset 11/93 (5042) and 7/94 (5043)		

5042 YAE 513V   5043 AFB 591V

5061-5062	Bristol VRT/SL3/6LXB; ECW	H43/31F
	Built 1978; ex Wilts & Dorset 5/94	

5061 VPR 484S   5062 VPR 485S

5101-5102	Volkswagen LT55; Optare	DP25F
	Built 1988; ex County Bus 10/93	

5101 E996 UYG   5102 E999 UYG

5103-5107	MCW MF150/108	B23F	Built 1989
	ex Wilts & Dorset 11/94(5103/4) and 4/95(5105-7)		

5103 F372 URU   5104 F373 URU   5105 F360 URU
5106 F361 URU   5107 F371 URU

5111	Freight Rover Sherpa; Carlyle	B20F
	Built 1987; ex Oakfield Travel 11/93	
5111 D79 TLV		

5121-5122	Freight Rover Sherpa; Steedrive(5121), Whittaker(5122)	
	Built 1985/9; ex Kimber 5/93	C16F

5121 C580 ABA   5122 F580 EWJ

5131-5132	Ford Transit; Dormobile	M16	Built 1982/1
	ex Oakfield Travel(5131) & Stoneman(5132) 11/93		

5131 XLF 32X   5132 VDD 276X

Tourist Coaches
Depot: Figheldean

6001	Leyland TRCTL11/2R; Duple	C53F	Built 1983
6001 YPD 124Y			

6011	Leyland PSU5B/4R; Duple	C55F	Built 1978
6011 OJI 1875 (previously AUS 644S)			

6021-6023	Bedford YMT; Duple (6021/2) and Plaxton (6023)		
	Built 1979/80/1	C53F	

6021 TCG 794T   6022 BAA 411V   6023 EFO 800W

6029	Ford R1114; Plaxton	C53F	Built 1980
6029 HFX 421V			

6031-6032	Volvo B58-61; Plaxton (6031) and Duple (6032)		
	Built 1980/2	C53F	

6031 LBC 555V   6032 TND 129X

6033-6034	Volvo B10M-61; Plaxton	C53F	Built 1985

6033 B873 XWR   6034 B874 XWR

6041	MAN SR280	C48FT	Built 1981
6041 HSV 342			

6051	Bedford SB5; Wadham Stringer	B34F	Built 1980
6051 TTA 827X			

6111	Freight Rover Sherpa; Carlyle	B20F	Built 1987
	ex Damory Coaches 2/95		
6111 D80 TLV			

6121	Toyota HB31R; Caetano Optima	C18F	Built 1989
6121 F659 YLJ			

6131	Mercedes 308D; Coachwork Walker	M15	Built 1989
6131 F423 RRD			

6132	Freight Rover Sherpa; Crystals	C16F	Built 1989
6132 G253 KET			

BODY CODES (before seating capacity)
B Single-deck bus   C Single-deck coach   M Minibus
H Double-deck bus with central upper deck gangway
DP Dual-purpose single-deck bus
O Permanent open-top double-deck bus
CO Convertible open-top double-deck bus

BODY CODES (after seating capacity)
F Front entrance   R Rear entrance   T Toilet-fitted